Praise for *Bait & Switch*

"Wondering, 'How did I get here?' in her exceptional book, *Bait & Switch*, international speaker Megan Hunter provides meaningful insight for people who sailed into love on a wave of excitement only to find themselves living inside a storm. She opens the doors to understanding what's happening beneath the surface with her explanation of the Complicated Operating System. This book is a must-read for anyone in love with a person with borderline personality traits making meaning out of the chaos while bringing skills and hope in an ocean of despair."

— Lynne Kenney, PsyD,
pediatric psychologist, international educator, and author of
The Family Coach Method and *Bloom: 50 Things to Say, Think, and Do
to Help Anxious, Angry, and Over the Top Kids*

"Megan Hunter has successfully tackled one of the biggest topics of today: What do you do when your great relationship turns into a struggle? She gives numerous practical tips on what you can do and how to influence your partner. She combines her experience and observations from working with hundreds of couples as an administrator for family court systems and as a business manager, to give the reader encouragement—and hope!"

— Bill Eddy, LCSW, Esq.,
president of the High Conflict Institute, and author of
*Splitting: Protecting Yourself While Divorcing Someone with Borderline
or Narcissistic Personality Disorder* and *So, What's Your Proposal?*

"In her book *Bait & Switch*, Megan Hunter addresses an important facet of parental relationships, and of our society in general: How can we handle, survive, and even thrive in relationships with a very difficult partner? That is, with partners who may be very attractive in some ways, yet have a personality skewed by a fear-based, threat-based view of the world. This personality issue renders relationships very challenging.

"Based on her years of experience in this field, Megan proposes an effective and simple strategy based on 'connecting, shifting, honesty, and consequences.' Connect with the emotional brain (right) to control the fire. Then shift to the analytic brain (left) to activate the thinking. This is something that we can all do and practice. Thank you Megan for articulating such a clear strategy that will help many of us."

— Frederic Bien, PhD,
President, Personality Disorder Awareness Network (PDAN.org)

"With extraordinary insight, Megan Hunter provides clear and usable strategies and skills for ending the chaos of high conflict relationships. Backed up by science, she provides the reader a detailed prescription for turning around behaviors and relationship patterns for the better. If you want to save your relationship, this book will show you how. If your relationship cannot be saved, this book will help you understand why, and provide you the groundwork for co-parenting after divorce and better relationships in the future, if that is where your path leads. This is a valuable piece of work."

— Angie Hallier,
Divorce Attorney, Fellow of the American Academy
of Matrimonial Lawyers, and author of *The Wiser Divorce –
Positive Strategies for your Next Best Life*

Saving Your Relationship
After Incredible Romance
Turns into Exhausting Chaos

Megan L. Hunter, MBA

UNHOOKED BOOKS
an imprint of High Conflict Institute Press
Scottsdale, Arizona

Copyright © 2015 by Megan L. Hunter
Unhooked Books, LLC
7701 E. Indian School Rd., Ste. F
Scottsdale, AZ 85251
www.unhookedbooks.com

ISBN: 978-1-936268-70-2 (paperback)
eISBN: 978-1-936268-71-9 (e-book)

Library of Congress Control Number: 2014952323

Cover Design: Gordan Blazevik
Interior Layout: Jeffrey Fuller

Printed in the United States of America

Dedicated to my husband Paul; to my beautiful children, Mychael and his wife Alison, Bryant, and Elizabeth; and to my teacher and mentor, Betsy Van Tuinen.

CONTENTS

PART II: CREATING A NEW ENVIRONMENT
TO MANAGE THE RELATIONSHIP

PREFACE

IN THE AUTUMN OF 2005, I HAPPENED ACROSS AN ARTICLE ABOUT HIGH-CONFLICT DIVORCE. I'd worked in divorce law long enough to know that these were the outlier cases—the seemingly impossible cases that were beyond what most would consider a "normal" divorce—they were family destroyers. These cases did not settle easily and often required a judge to decide every matter at issue. They usually took a year or more to be finalized and then ended up becoming "frequent filers," coming back to court to fight about anything and everything. These cases drained the budgets of the courts who adjudicated them, served as a source of frustration and helplessness for the professionals who handled them, and wiped out savings, retirement, and college funds for the high-conflict couple. But worst of all, the parents' behavior affected their children in damaging, disturbing ways.

Family law professionals share the notion that approximately 20 percent of family court cases consume around 80 percent of the court's time, energy, and resources, similar to the Pareto Principle. Most divorcing or separating spouses get through the process by settling it between themselves or by using mediation. Some need the assistance of professionals like lawyers, but they also eventually reach resolution. However, the approximately 20 percent of cases considered high conflict are those that keep lawyers, psychologists, therapists, social workers, and the courts busy. Indeed, high-conflict divorce and related child custody cases have created an unintended, thriving, multimillion-dollar, self-sustaining industry.

Families already in crisis typically seem to worsen in our adversarial court system. Some cases take years to litigate, with multiple attorneys and tens or even hundreds of thousands of dollars spent on lawyers for each parent, lawyers for the kids, psychologists, counselors, custody evaluators, parenting coordinators, and other professionals. Some custody evaluations can cost upward of ten thousand dollars. Long after the legal case is finally finished, the fighting continues as parents battle over co-parenting issues and everything else for years to come. More conflict, more loss, more drama, more chaos. **And: More damage to the kids and the parents!**

Although many jurisdictions in various countries have established programs to address this growing problem, their goal of helping parents reduce conflict and become more cooperative is often met with disappointing results. This phenomenon intrigued me. I wanted to know why a modern, sophisticated society with scores of intelligent, highly educated people working to solve this dilemma couldn't get this group to succeed with even the best educational, therapeutic, or other interventions.

So, back in 2005 when I read an article on high-conflict divorce called "How Personality Disorders Drive Family Court Litigation," by therapist/lawyer/mediator Bill Eddy, I experienced the ultimate "aha moment." Eddy, applying his therapy background to the dynamics of high-conflict family law cases, understood what was driving them—people who have personality disorders or traits of such disorders are usually involved. His logic opened the doors of understanding for me.

I invited Eddy to lead a training seminar for family court judges in my state, and again a few months later, to train mental health professionals who work with high-conflict cases doing psychological and custody evaluations. While originally thinking we would top out at thirty attendees, we finally had to close the doors at nearly two hundred participants. People wanted and needed to know how to help this outlier group.

This led me to the realization that people who work with family court cases were desperate to understand not only what made this population different from the other 80 percent of cases, but also how to effectively manage these cases. Shortly thereafter, I left my position at the Arizona Supreme Court Administrative Office of the Courts and convinced Bill Eddy to work with me to communicate his practical prescription for understanding and managing high-conflict family court cases to family law professionals everywhere. My business and family law background, combined with his expertise in all things high-conflict, proved highly successful. We jointly moved the needle forward in improving the lives of high-conflict families by training the professionals who deal with them.

Progress But Still Discontent

The court system is usually the end of the relationship road, and that frustrated me. Debate swirls around divorce statistics, but the reality is that at least half of the people in this stage of life—in which they cohabit, marry, divorce, remarry, and have children—will eventually come calling on the court to either dissolve the marriage, decide who gets custody of the kids, or determine how much time the kids will spend with the other parent.

Although the high-conflict industry provided my income, I had grown disillusioned being part of the clean-up crew.

While it was still satisfying to know we were helping move people through the court system with more ease (and thereby reducing the stress and frustration felt by professionals, as well as with decreasing the threat of lawsuits and complaints against their licenses), what kept nagging at me was an underlying belief about the population we were serving: that these were people who simply couldn't change and the only solution was to end the relationship.

Granted, many of these people displayed really ugly behavior and seemingly deserved the labels they were commonly given—"crazy," "psycho," "psycho bitch," "lunatic," "borderline," "narcissist," "sociopath," or "psychopath." Typically, only the most patient people, usually mental health professionals, had any success in dealing with them. Most others eventually learned to avoid them because the very thought of dealing with or even being around them was too distressing. It's true; they're exhausting to deal with or be around. Some of us find ourselves in constant conflict with them, while the rest of us just try to run away from them.

However, the more I studied human behavior, particularly the brain's role in relationships and conflict, the more wasteful it seemed. I asked myself: Was a segment of society incapable of having successful relationships? Could relationships be saved if at least one partner understood the brain nature of this relationship impairment? Could divorce or relationship dissolution be avoided if at least one person took ownership of managing the relationship in a skillful way? What would happen if they had the right set of instructions for this particular brain; if they understood their own brain's unconscious reactions?

Through the years I've worked to help many individuals develop the skills to manage an ongoing relationship with their ex-spouse or ex-partner, typically because they share children. Circling back six months or even a year later, I asked about their successes and mistakes. Most reported varying degrees of success as they practiced using their new skills during interactions with their former partner. The more they practiced, the better they got. My final interview question was this: "If you had these skills while you were still together, do you think the relationship might have survived and you would have an intact family today?" Many, but not all agreed that their relationship troubles may have had a more positive outcome with the knowledge and skills they now possessed. Sadly, no one has reported a desire to reconcile—the wounds are too deep. While my anecdotal evidence is not a scientific study, my findings were informative and prompted me to write this book.

Now, in addition to my continuing work helping professionals understand and manage these cases differently, I also focus my energy on what happens **before** a couple makes the decision to file for divorce or otherwise end the relationship. I've been frustrated knowing that many, not all, couples want to stay together, but can't seem to make it work—even if they've read loads of relationship books and gone to counseling. Their relationship continues swirling in chaos until it ends.

I deal with couples who have the most extreme and dreadful relationships, but the strategies and solutions I advocate also work for those with less conflict and adversity. My current passion and commitment is to focus on giving all these people hope, not only for saving their relationship, but also for rebuilding loving, trusting partnerships that have the potential to endure.

INTRODUCTION

As you pick up this book, are you lost in a relationship nightmare, one that has become chaotic, complicated, and extreme? Does your partner constantly demand your attention and need to feel connected to you most or all of the time by phone, text, or email when you're apart? Do you get blamed for every argument? Did your relationship start with an intense spark that later turned into chaos? Do you deal with jealousy about your friends, extended family, or co-workers? Defensiveness? Do arguments sometimes become out-of-control explosions? Do items get thrown? Does your partner sometimes storm out of the room, slamming doors? Do you feel confused and overwhelmed about what to do?

If you answered yes to any of these questions, this book is written to help you. This book is about what I call "bait and switch" relationships. These are relationships that begin with a flurry of romance and intensity (the bait) and at some point undergo a radical transformation (the switch). After the switch is thrown, the relationship is characterized by extreme behaviors, and a sense of great instability and chaos. While the relationships may not include all of the behaviors listed above or may differ from those listed, the type of behaviors and interactions we'll be discussing all fall outside of the range expected in a normal relationship and indicate that the relationship is at high risk of falling apart.

Note: Some relationships are so toxic that ending it may be the best solution. If yours is violent, abusive, or potentially violent, it's best to do a risk assessment and seek safety. You are not helping yourself or your partner by allowing abuse. I would like to take the easy route by declining to address abuse and violence; however, a key feature of some of these relationships is a lack of impulse control mixed with extreme pain that shows itself as rage. The combination can and often does result in violence or some sort. I do not hold myself out as an expert on domestic violence or abuse; however, I have been involved for most of my career in listening to all sides of domestic violence in crafting policy and legislation to address it in the courts and training others about how to deal with it in the professional realm and in individual relationships. So I choose to address the reality of relationships such as these. It is required. You will find that I do not advocate putting up with abuse or violence of any kind, but I also do not see it as entirely all-or-nothing. The skills in this book are meant to help you manage the relationship differently to reduce the chaos and thus, the incidence of violence. If, after reading this paragraph (or even the entire book), you are confused about what to do about your abusive relationship, please seek outside help. The Resource section lists several resources for you to turn to.

Anecdotally, about 10-15 percent of people in marriages or other romantic relationships have experienced much of these behaviors. Most of these relationships end badly in divorce court or long, drawn-out break-ups that destroy families and are usually devastating in every way. These are the *War of the Roses* relationships that you don't talk about casually over the water cooler or the backyard fence, because no one could fathom—or believe—what you're going through.

In the past, there was no hope for these relationships. The

behaviors involved just seemed too extreme, the problems too complex, and failure and dissolution appeared to be the only way out. I've witnessed this innumerable times in my work in family law, as a trainer of professionals who handle high-conflict divorce and child custody cases, and my work with individuals and couples. By the time I'm contacted for help, it's usually too late for the relationship to survive; one partner has pending criminal charges or may be in jail, there is an alleged false accusation, the court won't allow contact with the kids due to accusations of domestic violence or child abuse, or one partner has the feeling of being trapped and is simply overwhelmed. Divorce or some type of break-up seems to be the only option.

Another Way Out of the Chaos

I think it's important to pause and remember that the person before you now, the person who is making your life feel unruly and out of control, is the same person you fell in love with sometime in the past. Even though this layer of awfulness seems unconquerable, on some level you believe there may still be a good person inside. Your friends, family, colleagues, pastor/priest, therapist, and just about any sensible person who knows your story will likely tell you to RUN. Yet, I firmly believe that many of these relationships can be saved with understanding, training, discipline, and practice.

The first thing you need to know about me is that I have tremendous compassion and empathy for both of the people caught in the chaos. I also feel immensely frustrated when these relationships end simply because one or both partners do not know what to do. These are extreme relationships, with extremely intense people, who may leave you feeling like there's no alternative, and worse yet, no hope. They're outside the norm—outliers. Although many relationship experts and therapists don't hold out much hope for these relationships, I'm different. I believe that many, not all, have a chance at surviving, and even have a chance at happiness, if you—the person who has the ability to manage the relationship—get educated and develop a new skill set for interacting with your partner.

It's not easy, and it depends largely on how "hooked" you are—that is, your unconscious response to conflict. The more you unhook from your customary behavior and responses, the easier it will be to do the opposite of what you're used to doing, and the more success you'll have in turning the relationship around. There are no guarantees or promises of success, but there are some strategies you can try. After all, you've already invested a lot of time and effort into this relationship, and you may even have children together, which makes splitting up inherently more difficult. It's worth a shot trying to save the relationship.

In this book, we'll talk about how bait and switch relationships develop, examine the factors that lead to extreme relationship behaviors, and explore specific strategies and skills you can use to restore your relationship to health and sustain it over the long term.

One of the most important ideas we'll explore is that relationships are all about the brain—the stuff going on that we know, see, and control, and the unseen stuff that causes these relationship disorders. Today we know much about how the brain works and how it affects our behavior. We'll talk about the science of the brain in these pages and consider how this knowledge may provide answers for resolving relationship issues.

Just as there have been advances in understanding how the brain works in people with various brain differences like autism or traumatic brain injuries, we have learned that some people's brains function a little differently when it comes to relationships and human interaction. We are beginning to understand that we can't use the same strategies in these relationships with the expectation of having a successful relationship. We keep doing the same thing in them but expecting different result. Sounds like insanity. It's like chasing your tail, except the tail eventually gets bitten off. I've come to realize that the ultimate act of empathy is adapting your own actions in order to help another human being improve theirs.

That's what this book is about. First, understanding what's going on in your partner's brain, then what's going on in yours. Then, learning about and being disciplined enough to modify or adapt your reactions and responses even when you don't feel like doing it or want to do it. When you shift in this way, the chaos will calm, you will feel more confident, less stressed and less confused.

Building Relationship Intelligence

It's important to point out that this is not a book meant to demonize the person who seems to be destroying a relationship. What you'll learn is that they are directed by an internal operating system of such strong magnitude that it drives them to behaviors that feel normal to them, although they are viewed as extreme behaviors outside what is considered the norm for healthy relationships. These actions are neither their own choosing, nor are they aware that they even have this operating system. Let's call it "relationship impairment." These are people who have an immense capacity to love, be amazing parents, compassionate friends, and even have great jobs. They're not bad people with no hope. They're good people with a different operating system who can interact better when those closest to them know the successful interactions to use. That is relationship intelligence.

Heroes and Villains

So, let's have an understanding from the beginning that you are not the hero and your partner is not the villain. Because your world feels chaotic, it can be difficult to find empathy. Let's think about it in a different way: Let's say that you've been in love with your partner for several years and you have a strong relationship. One day your partner gets hurt in a bicycle accident, and even though your partner survived, a part of the brain will never again be the same—the part that regulates emotion. The doctors tell you that he or she will experience unpredictable mood swings that you will have to be prepared to address as they happen. The smart, clever, funny, charming, witty features are still there, but you will now have this challenging feature to contend with going forward. What do you think about this? Would you automatically flee the relationship? Or would you adjust your thinking, learning everything you can to adapt your behavior, and realize that life is going to be different going forward? The answer is likely a simple one: you will need to adapt your reactions and responses to accommodate these new limitations. Would you love your partner any less because of this brain impairment?

Think about romantic relationship (where there has been no traumatic intervening event) in the same way. This is where people get stuck. Because this chaotic relationship is so far outside the norm, we don't know what to do, so we do what we know to do, and what we're used to doing in our relationships with most people. We become combative, react in ways we're not proud of, say things we don't mean, become too directive telling our partner what to do (even though they rarely take our advice), and avoid the situation or the person. When that doesn't work (which it won't), we feel hopeless. Everything we've tried seems to fail. Your partner doesn't improve or change even though there were promises to change. Worse yet, your partner may not even acknowledge there is any need to change or even that there is a problem. So we eventually succumb to the exhaustion, declare defeat, and head to dissolution land.

Many (maybe most) of these relationships end simply because we don't understand what we're facing and don't know how to deal with it. I've never been a person who is content with allowing others to flounder in misery when solutions are available. You need to understand what you're dealing with, and understand how hooked you really are. You'll like the "Are You Hooked" test. I am also confident you'll like to learn how to unhook and how to manage the relationship differently in order for your partner to have any chance at having a successful relationship with you.

Nothing is a certainty in life—far from it. What we're dealing with here are the most difficult "difficult" relationships, which means they have the highest risk of failure. No one— not me, nor any who reads this book—can be assured that a high-conflict relationship will be saved. However, I hope that through education and understanding, we will begin to see more relationships saved than lost.

A Note about Personality Disorders and Relationship Difficulties

In our society is a mental health diagnosis called Borderline Personality Disorder (BPD). It is a seriously painful disorder to the sufferer, who may not know they have it, thus leaving it largely untreated for many. If you've read about it, you already know that it's viewed as a "scary" disorder. It's widely viewed as untreatable, although in reality it is treatable in varying degrees and successes.

It's also a serious relationship disruptor. Generally, BPD can be separated into two categories: introverts and extroverts, with the latter being addressed in this book. An extrovert does not know they operate differently in relationships than other people. As you will read in this book, it's all about how the brain developed from the very beginning.

Writing about BPD is a bit tricky and risky. I do not wish to perpetuate the labeling of any person, especially with something that has serious negative connotations associated with it. However, it is a reality that should be recognized in our society and given the respect and support it deserves and requires.

I take the position that:

- many relationships are destroyed because of this undetected disorder
- the disorder is much more pervasive in society than statistics are able to identify
- many people suffer because we refuse to talk about it until it's too late to save a relationship
- many relationships can be saved with knowledge, empathy, and new skills

This book is not meant to be a compendium on BPD nor is it intended to serve as a treatment source or final word on BPD. Instead, it is based on the premise that many relationship break-downs follow a similar pattern—one that shares features with BPD. Thus, this book focuses on how to use education and new skills to help your loved one and help yourself—not label, demonize, or castigate them in any way.

It's time to unveil the mysteries of BPD and stop perpetuating the myth that people who suffer with it cannot be in successful and happy relationships.

Many books on this topic are hidden from the person presumed to have BPD or high-conflict. This one strives to be different. It recognizes the value of every human being and acknowledges the pain that they must unwittingly endure. It separates the brain process from the person, helping us shift from confusion and judgment to empathy and understanding.

Disclaimer: I am not saying that every person who reads this book is in love with someone who may have BPD. I am saying that it could be the case and if it is, here are some tips on how to handle it.

Recommendations for books and other resources on BPD are listed in the Resource section.

PART I

Understanding
the Relationship Brain

CHAPTER 1

Trajectory from Incredible Romance to Exhausting Chaos

Author note: Gender is used interchangeably throughout this book.

I f only I'd collected a dollar from every client who, in an exhausted voice, starts the conversation with (and usu ally they're either whispering or loudly ranting), "You have absolutely no idea what a nightmare I'm living. Other people may have some pretty awful relationship war stories, but, believe me, you've never heard anything like this. I've looked the devil in the eye and barely survived. I think my partner has a chemical imbalance—probably bipolar."

There is no point in telling them I've heard the same thing countless times from countless people. Really, we could just skip the entire story part and go straight to the "what to do" part, but we don't. Instead, I give them my full atten-tion and listen to their account of the relationship terrorist (their words) to whom they have given their heart. For some, it's the first time they've dared utter their story out loud. For others, it is the first time anyone has listened and un-derstood—a validating experience that brings relief. The stories all have similar elements and patterns.

Exhausting Chaos Stories

"She threatens, manipulates, and controls me, and I can't

tell you how many times she's thrown her wedding ring out the window. When I'm with her, we can have the most amazing time together, but as soon as I go to work, hang out with my friends, stop by my parents' house, have an important board meeting—anything—she has an emergency and does everything in her power to get me to come home so I can fix it and make her feel better. Sometimes it works and then we go back to a somewhat calm norm. I may even get a tearful apology. Many times it doesn't work and we end up going in endless circles until I want to scream or head straight out the door. It almost seems intentional—to the point of sabotage—but it's hard to imagine anyone intentionally behaving this way."

"It's a rare day when we do not have an argument. Some days are simply exhausting. Others are rage and chaos. I'm nearing my breaking point. I could give her a million dollars, buy her an estate on the French Riviera complete with a Maserati in the garage, and give her 100% of my time, but she'd still be unhappy, complain about it, and blame me for ruining her life. She says I don't include her in my life; she doesn't feel accepted by me or my family and friends; and that I make her feel bad. Most conversations start with the phrase 'you' and finish with the list of ways I've screwed up and made her miserable."

"When we argue, it's almost as if every word I say is sliced in half by her verbal sword. No matter how much I try to explain my point of view or try to get her to understand something seemingly logical, I lose. Even walking away to help calm the situation seems to amp it up instead of wind it down."

"At first, it was totally shocking, but I was able to forgive her behavior and move on. Over time, however, I've realized that it always goes back to 'awful' even though I know what to watch for now and how to structure my life to avoid these disruptions. She still manages to catch me by surprise and propel my world into the darkest depths. It sort of goes from heaven to hell; light to dark; calm to storm; all good to all bad. I'm the best, and then I'm the worst. It's like living in opposite worlds but never knowing which world to anticipate at any given time. She's destroying my health, my finances, my family, my job. Soon I'll have nothing left, and even though I love her, it's becoming clear that I don't have a clue how to make this work."

"She's threatened to have me thrown in jail for abuse or to 'expose' me for the fraud I am to my company. Even though I know I haven't abused her or anyone, nor have I defrauded my company, she's so convincing and so emotional about it that I'm afraid others might believe her. She can be the most vindictive person, and then be completely kind, gentle, and sweet to someone else in the next breath."

"The worst times are when she threatens to hurt herself or says she feels like dying, which usually happens right when I have something major going on—like an important meeting (causing me to choose between the two) or a family gathering (which she refuses to attend because my family treats her so bad)."

"It's a horrible feeling to be responsible for someone else's life and happiness; it feels like a full-time job. I want both of us to be happy, but everything I do seems to backfire."

"I'm not getting any sleep because I'm worried that she will either attack me or hurt herself. Other times she wakes me in the night to talk about our relationship—again. Honestly, I just want to run far, far away. I don't know how much more I can take of the chaos, but I feel completely trapped and isolated. If I stay, my life is hell and she doesn't get better.

If I leave, I worry that she won't survive even though my gut says these are just threats. I feel torn between my parents and my wife because she wants me to side with her against them."

"I'm exhausted."

Does this Trajectory Really Happen?

While we want to believe that relationships like this only happen in the movies, or to people we see on the news, or in an episode of *48 Hours,* in actuality they are shockingly common and seem to be on the rise. Notwithstanding the stories reflected above, people generally don't talk about being in such chaotic relationships, not even to their closest friends or family, either because they are embarrassed or because they don't think anyone would believe them. After all, it sounds so incredibly outlandish—plus, their partner would "cream them" if they found out they had told others. It seems to be an impossible dilemma. However, if you're in this kind of relationship, you likely know exactly what I'm talking about.

The scenarios I've described above may be extreme examples, but they unfortunately are not uncommon. Though some high-conflict relationships are somewhat more subtle and less extreme, they still follow a similar pattern of chaos and relationship sabotage and will benefit from the same strategies.

Incredible Romance

After reflecting on the disturbing stories about the romantic relationship evolving into a series of exhausting and chaotic interactions, we need to back up to the beginning and look at how these relationships get started. No one intentionally seeks a romantic partner who will make life miserable, so how and why does it happen? It usually starts like this:

"At the beginning, we had the most incredibly intense spark! He was charming, sweet, nice, funny, and totally adaptable. In fact, he was so adaptable that he seemed to just blend right into my life—the perfect match. We had the same hobbies, likes and dislikes, tastes in music and movies. Basically, everything I liked to do, he liked to do. My dreams were his dreams. My goals were his goals. We were totally and absolutely compatible and in sync."

"He understood my personality, my character, my emotions, and my ambitions. He was supportive of my career and my relationships. We had fun. We traveled. We fell in love so completely and quickly—it went from zero to sixty in the blink of an eye. Within days, he was spending nights at my place, and even began leaving things like his toothbrush at my house. Our sex life was intense. It wasn't long before we were living together, although we had never actually discussed it. Even though it seemed a little fast, it just felt good and it was so intense. He was completely available, romantic, and met my needs in every way. Rose petal trails from the front door to my bedroom, champagne, romantic trips. It was the best time of my life!"

The Spark and Chemistry

Many describe an intense spark at first meeting—something that we believe indicates we've met "the one." That spark has the power to override our sensibilities and convince us to ignore any and all red flags. Some people describe it as chemistry. "We have amazing chemistry!" "The chemistry between us is unmistakable, something I've never felt before!"

Unfortunately, we mistakenly identify the spark and chemistry as a positive and confirmatory sign of future relationship success when in reality it should serve as a yield or warning sign—a sign to slow down and take things one step at a time. I'm not saying that every spark is wrong—just that it *might* point to problems down the road with a particular personality type. The "spark" might well mean caution. "Chemistry" might be a red flag.

So what causes a seemingly amazing relationship to turn into a nightmare?

Bait and Switch

Often, the type of relationship described in the various stories calls to mind a marketing term used in the business world—the "bait and switch." It is the promise or experience of something or someone highly desirable that eventually turns that something or someone almost the complete opposite of the expectation or promise.

Most long-term relationships experience ups and downs and a gradual shift from the romance of dating to the less exciting everyday life of marriage. With the bait and switch relationship, the shift is usually more sudden and extreme.

I recently saw an example of this on the reality television series *True Tori*. This show looked into the private life of actress Tori Spelling (whose father, Aaron Spelling, was one of the most successful and wealthiest film and television producers) and her husband, Dean. After doing a few reality shows about their love life, marriage, and growing family over the years, Dean was caught, very publicly, in an extramarital affair while he was working in Canada while Tori and their children were going about their daily lives back in California. True Tori was created to capture their journey attempting to recover from this relationship disaster. In their previous reality shows, all was wonderful, silly, romantic, and lovely, but the new post-affair show revealed a different story about their marriage. Tori detailed for the millions of viewers watching the worst part of their lives, the sudden switch from the romantic husband (with whom she'd fallen in love, trusted, and married) to the reality of a very different person—almost immediately after the vows. She actually used the phrase "bait and switch" when speaking about the sudden transition after they married. Interestingly, Dean said much the same about her.

Often, not always, the switch from good to bad happens when the relationship becomes permanent in some way, for example, when the couple moves in together or gets married. In my experience, this bait and switch phenomenon is a common thread in these very difficult relationships although some happen more gradually over time. Let's just say that at some point the relationship goes from really, really good to really, really awful. You're in shock and awe because it was so incredibly good in the beginning. When the disruptions occur, you're taken by surprise. Then the tears and apologies come . . . things even out for a while . . . until the next troubling episode.

Lisa's Bait and Switch Story

During college, Lisa fell in love with another student, Peter. Their relationship developed quickly—the couple was soon spending every waking moment together or at least thinking about each other, giving each other romantic cards or flowers, going on dates to concerts and games, or just hanging out. She felt a magical, intense spark when they were together, which she took as a good sign.

She met Peter's family, who seemed quite normal, nice, and accepting of her. His best pals from childhood were still his closest friends. He did well in school, excelled in his studies, and appeared to be headed toward a fulfilling career and marriage. It's true that he was kind of a jerk sometimes, but she passed that off to his background of being around a bunch of guys who liked to give each other a hard time. They quickly got engaged and had a lovely wedding. Two days later, Peter was screaming expletives at her through the phone because she was late coming home from dropping off some things to one of her bridesmaids. He called her what even the most foul-mouthed would consider the very worst and degrading names a woman can be called. As Lisa listened, she stood immobilized in the living room of her friend's home, tears streaming down her face, unsure what to do. She was devastated, demoralized and taken completely aback. Embarrassed and scared, she rushed home to her new husband and to a life that would never be the same. Her confidence quickly eroded, and she devoted herself to making Peter happy and avoiding a repeated event. Sometimes her efforts worked and sometimes they didn't.

Eventually she reached her limit and began fighting back, which ultimately led to divorce. Interestingly, Peter had never erupted in such a way prior to their marriage.

Beyond the Switch

This book is not about the actual bait or the switch. If you're reading this, you are likely well past that stage and are embroiled in exhausting chaos, trying to figure out how to make your relationship work. So that's what we will focus on—what to do at this point in the type of relationship that I like to call the **Complicated Relationship**. We'll discuss tools and strategies to help you save your relationship and improve daily life for you and your partner (and your kids, if you have them). Conversely, we'll discuss how to exit the relationship safely if you deem that is the best move for your particular situation.

As mentioned previously, all relationships have ups and downs, conflict and misunderstandings. The **Complicated Relationship**, however, is one that falls outside the normal range of relationship behaviors. Take some time to work through the test below to determine whether you are in one.

EXERCISE: Identifying the Complicated Relationship

How do you know if you're in a Complicated Relationship? The following list describes traits typically found in a complicated relationship. Think of your relationship and place a checkmark next to the traits that apply to your partner. This exercise is about identifying *patterns of behavior* to determine if you are in a complicated relationship. One-time incidents or events do not qualify.

_____ 1. An inability to handle feedback or criticism well and tendency to be overly defensive

_____ 2. Sees him or herself as the victim and you as the one at fault ("you always . . ." or " you never . . .")

_____ 3. Believes that you never satisfies his or her needs

_____ 4. Jealous of your relationships with family, friends, or colleagues

_____ 5. Overly sexual in the beginning; may use sex as a weapon later

_____ 6. Goes from calm to rage in a split second; may throw things, hit, or scratch you

_____ 7. Isolates

_____ 8. Quickly jumps to conclusions

_____ 9. Quickly flips from idealizing people to cutting them from his or her life

_____ 10. Usually yells or raises voice when upset or curses outside his or her norm; mood swings

_____ 11. Uses words like abandoned, rejected, unwelcome, attention

_____ 12. Feels entitled to read your email, text messages, personal mail, or phone history

_____ 13. Threatens to or actually harms self, e.g. banging head on wall, hitting face or body, jumping out of moving vehicle, etc.

_____ 14. Won't let go of the past, an old fight, or something he or she believes you've done to them

_____ 15. Self-medicates with alcohol, prescription, or non-prescription drugs to calm self when upset

_____ 16. Punishes, retaliates, or becomes vindictive; makes attacks very personal

How did you score? If you checked four or more items, this indicates that you are probably in a **complicated relationship**, and one or both of you may have what I call a **"Complicated Operating System."** Each relationship will have different experiences, but the behaviors above are commonly associated with the complicated relationships this book addresses.

Levels of Complication: Test Scores

Between 1-4

If you checked four or less, your relationship has some issues that should be addressed. This book is filled with tips to help you build awareness and then modify and practice new behaviors. The risk of relationship failure is on the lower end.

Between 5-9

If you checked anywhere from five to nine, you are in a complicated relationship at high risk of continuing chaos and failure without intervention.

Ten or more

If you checked most or all of the items, you are at the extreme end of a complicated relationship, which is characterized by extreme emotions, behaviors, anxiety, and actions. This would be considered a highly complicated relationship that has a high risk of failure without intervention and change.

Hope and Deep Reserves of Empathy: Understanding the Complicated Operating System and Getting Unhooked

Don't give up hope if your relationship is complicated. That's what this book is about. We'll discuss strategies that, when practiced with discipline and care, can help you build a healthier, more loving relationship with your partner. The work involved will require you to override your established habits and patterns when it comes to what you do and how you feel. Essentially, you'll need to learn to do the opposite. It requires knowing your commitment level and love for your partner and holding on to that through even the toughest of times. And, most important, it requires an understanding that your partner is not intentionally trying to sabotage you or your relationship. Equally important, you need to understand that your partner is suffering from an insidious, hidden brain process that he or she doesn't even know is abnormal. You'll need to draw on deep reserves of empathy.

Taking the first steps toward a new way of interacting with your partner becomes possible only with an understanding of the reasons for his or her behavior and each partner's conscious and unconscious predictable interactions. In the first chapters, you will learn about the "complicated operating system," how and why the complicated brain works this way, as well as your own conflict response style (how and why you react the way you do). In the remaining chapters, you'll learn how to **"unhook"** from the things you're doing that aren't working, how to enhance the things you do that are working, and how to develop new skills for reducing conflict and changing unhealthy relationship dynamics.

Seeing Yourself as Complicated

After taking the test, you may have discovered that you have a few of the described characteristics. We all do to some degree. With this insight, you have the opportunity to work on your own behaviors.

If you scored in the higher range of the test, you may already realize that you struggle with relationships. Perhaps you even see yourself as the partner driving the "complicated" part of the relationship. If you recognize some of your behaviors in the list, that's a good thing and a great start. It means you have some work to do and that there is hope for your relationship. Don't give up or convince yourself that you are beyond being helped. Just take it for what it is and trust that through your reading of this book, you can understand the reasons for some of your behaviors and how you can change them. There is no judgment in these pages; only strategies for healing. If you continue reading, you will discover that your brain developed in a certain way that makes relationships difficult for you. This wasn't your doing. You didn't ask for it, and you don't want it. However, just as a person with some type of brain injury from an accident didn't ask for it, they still have to deal with it.

This may be upsetting news, but if you are open to accepting that there is a tried-and-true prescription for turning around your behaviors and relationship patterns, you are more likely to reduce your anxiety, achieve relationship success, and just feel a whole lot better.

Some people experience a grieving period when they discover that they are more "complicated" than they previously realized, or that they're in a complicated relationship. It's not the end of the world. Rather, it's a first step toward a new and better life. Keep reading, take lots of notes, make an appointment with a good therapist, and give yourself some grace for being you as you learn about the Complicated Operating System and how to transform it, and your relationship.

CHAPTER 2

The Relationship Operating System: It's "Complicated"

Think about the way people describe difficult romantic relationships. You'll often hear them say, "It's complicated," and you may have even said that about your own relationship. "Complicated" has many meanings to different people—it could mean a long-distance relationship, an age difference, financial disparities, or other romance difficulties.

When I think about difficult relationships, those that are seemingly hopeless, chaotic and exhausting, I call them "complicated relationships," in which one or both people have a "Complicated Operating System" (Complicated OS™).

What exactly is a Complicated OS and how did it develop? This chapter introduces you to the concept of patterned operating rules within ourselves where systems are healthy, complicated, or somewhere in between.

Note: If you did not take the "Identifying the Complicated Relationship" quiz at the end of chapter 1, take a few minutes to go through it now, so you can understand whether you are in a complicated relationship before reading on. This chapter will make a lot more sense if you do.

The Relationship Operating System™

We can think about our need to be in romantic relationships, the way we behave in them, and our ability to sustain such relationships as being controlled by an operating system of sorts, what I call a "relationship operating system." This system governs what we do and how we behave in relationships, particularly when it comes to our need or desire to be in a romantic relationship and how we handle conflict within it. Our operating system is essentially a set of rules, one that began developing early in life, which influence how we interact with other people. Although everyone is an individual with unique looks, temperament, and personality, we each have a different set of rules that predict and govern how we operate in relationships.

This relationship operating system is similar to the inner workings (operating system) of a computer. Think about your own computer. It's probably either a Mac with an operating system developed by Apple, or a PC using a Windows-based operating system.

The computer's operating system is programmed with a set of rules that tell the computer what to do. Programmers develop the rules to make the computer operate in a certain way. Whether the rules of a computer's operating system work the way we expect depends on our particular needs, whether any design or equipment flaws exist, how we treat and take care of the computer, and whether we get any viruses or bugs in the system or damage to the parts.

When we look at a computer, regardless of whether it's a Mac or a PC, we instantly know it is a computer and that it will help us in our work or personal lives. Most of us don't really care what kind of operating system it has; we just want it to function and work well when we need it. I think the same can be said for relationships.

IT professionals know there are pros and cons to computer operating systems. For example, some operating systems are more user-friendly than others, some require less maintenance, and some offer better security and higher productivity. Likewise, our relationship operating systems intrinsically include different qualities and attributes, strengths and weaknesses. Simply put, some of us operate like Macs and others like PCs.

It's easy to overlook this concept. While our intuition and experience tell us that people have differing abilities to be successful in relationships, in most cases we don't give it more than a cursory consideration. We don't stop to think about what it means that some people are governed by a different set of internal rules for relationship behavior, until you find yourself in an exhausting, chaotic relationship without a clue about how you got there.

Unfortunately, this is where we go wrong. It's where our expectations are flawed.

In the relationship realm, we have the same expectations of relationship behavior for nearly everyone we meet. We think if we're a Mac, almost everyone we meet is a Mac, unless they give us a reason to think they're a sociopath or complete weirdo. Further, we mistakenly assume we can use the same techniques and strategies to form and navigate relationships with just about anyone. We mistakenly apply our own logic and relationship behaviors to other people.

Because relationship operating systems are internal, we have no way of immediately knowing what system we're dealing with—just as we can't tell from a computer's shell whether it uses a Windows or Mac operating system, or even UNIX or Linux. You're playing a game without all the pieces.

Now you may be better able to understand why that seductive spark or amazing chemistry we have with some people should be a warning signal instead of a green light!

This example may provide insight:

While I was in grad school, my fiancé took me on a trip to Europe for the Christmas holidays to meet his daughter and son-in-law who were living in Luxembourg. My grad school course was online, giving me the ability to submit work from anywhere in the world wherever there was Internet access. A fairly large paper was due on Christmas Eve during the trip that didn't get completed before we left, so I had to finish it in Luxembourg. Well, as it went, my laptop stopped working, leaving me to use my future stepdaughter's computer. As I typed along on her computer, I noticed that many of the words were misspelled. Thinking my fingers were on the wrong keys, I started over. Imagine my surprise when I realized that several keys on the computer keyboard were in different places from the American keyboard I was used to using. As I typed, I continued hitting the keys where I expected them to be, but the result was the creation of a new and unintelligible language. I felt frustration and panic. My expectations were flawed, and I was taken by surprise. I had the same expectations for the European keyboard that I'd experienced with my American keyboard. I'd lived my entire life thinking there was only one type of keyboard with all the keys in the same place, and now I had to adjust to a different keyboard. It certainly wasn't going to adjust to me. You might say the keyboard was "complicated." It wasn't bad—just different.

It's difficult to wrap our heads around two operating systems and truly understand what they mean. Is it just that people are different? No, it's much deeper and more insidious.

Complicated versus Healthy Operating Systems

It comes down to this simple piece of information—some people have a healthy Relationship Operating System and some have a complicated Relationship Operating System. We all fall somewhere within a continuum from healthy to "complicated." How do we know if a person is healthy or complicated? Let's face it, we don't walk around with a sign advertising our ability to be a healthy romantic partner, nor does our relationship status on Facebook accurately indicate whether we are a relationship genius or relationship impaired.

Wouldn't it be nice if we came with a set of instructions that told us exactly how much we—or our partners—needed to be "relationship healthy" and what missing or lacking ingredients would help us achieve that status?

The simple way to think about complicated versus healthy relationships is to go back to the quiz from Chapter 1. All of the items in that questionnaire are features of the Complicated OS: overly defensive, overly sensitive or emotional, mood swings, raging, punishing (vindictive), black and white thinking, and others. Now, swap those behaviors with the exact opposite behaviors. The person with a healthy operating system is not overly defensive or overly sensitive. They don't rage. They can regulate their emotions, see gray areas, formulate options, and find middle ground in relationships.

Remember, not every complicated person has all features from the quiz and not every person with a healthy operating system is completely free of some of them either. However, the Complicated OS is one in which a **pattern of behavior** with these features is present on a **continuing basis**, especially in the romantic relationship.

The pattern involves the constant need for relationship and how they choose partners, and how they behave within the relationship once they're in one. While it seems unpredictable and chaotic, it's actually quite predictable. The good news is the more you understand the predictable patterns, expect and watch for them, the less chaotic your life will be.

Impact on Other Areas of Life and Intention

Grasping this new concept and new reality can be difficult to comprehend and accept because you may see your partner as an intelligent person who can get along with other people, get a degree and maybe even an advanced degree, hold a job, volunteer with abused animals, be kind to children, and come across as a logical person. It's hard to comprehend that this functioning, attractive, smart person is not *intentionally* destroying your relationship and causing you lots of problems. The venom and hostility that can spew forth from your partner likely leads you to believe that he or she absolutely knows what they're doing and is thereby intentional.

It's not. Your partner is a person with a Complicated OS who experiences high anxiety and fear-based thinking when it comes to relationships, particularly romantic ones. In the coming chapters we explore the inner workings of the brain that cause these behaviors. Your understanding will increase and with understanding will come empathy, a non-negotiable requirement when dealing with a person with a

---

[1]Vanderbilt University, 2011.

Complicated OS. You will discover that your empathy is the first step to reducing the chaos.

Summary

Everyone has a Relationship Operating System; the way we behave in relationships. Each person is somewhere along a continuum of that Relationship Operating System of healthy or "complicated". Relationships that follow a pattern of behavior that include an absolute need to be in a romantic relationship to feel like they can breathe, along with specific behaviors within it that create chaos are defined as having a Complicated Operating System.

In the next two chapters we will explore the two main elements of the complicated OS:

1) the intense need to be in a romantic relationship

2) how we behave within that relationship once we have one.

CHAPTER 3

The Complicated Operating System: Desperate Need for Relationships

What sets the Complicated OS apart from the healthy OS? Two factors differentiate them:

1) how we choose relationship partners, and

2) how we behave within relationships.

This chapter discusses how we choose relationship partners and the need to be in a relationship. How we behave once a relationship is formed is addressed in Chapter 4.

The Desire and Need for Relationships

Hermits notwithstanding, most people desire to be in love and to share life with a companion. We can all think of people who are in stable, happy, lasting relationships, and others who hop from one relationship to the next, constantly dissatisfied and determinedly seeking another. Others seem content to remain single until the right person comes along. Have you wondered what makes people so different?

Most of us base our romantic choices on several factors: physical attraction, compatibility (shared interests), a spark, chemistry, a desire to have a family, geographical proximity, and others. Or, we simply fall for someone. Let's call these criteria the *first dimension* in romantic relationships. They are important, but they don't tell us the whole story. Watch an episode or two of the reality dating shows *The Bachelor* or *The Bachelorette,* or any romantic movie, and you'll see and hear these as the criteria for our romantic partnership choices. Think about your relationships and the qualities that drew you in. More than likely, these criteria were involved.

Ultimately, most of us find love through a spark or chemistry topped off with compatibility.

Compatibility

We meet people in many ways. Maybe you met your partner on an airplane, at work, at church, or a neighbor's backyard barbecue. Wherever you met, you probably felt compatible in at least a few ways. In the last decade or so, dating websites have become an increasingly popular place to meet people. Sites like Match.com and others bring people together based on various factors like looks and similar interests. It's like picking a partner from a catalog. Another dating site, eHarmony, found its success by developing a compatibility method. Their members answer questionnaires about beliefs, values, emotional health, skills, and other characteristics, which the eHarmony algorithm matches them with potentially compatible people.

eHarmony's vice president of Matching, Steve Carter, presented a paper at the sixteenth annual American Psychological Society meeting where he summarized the results of a study they conducted to measure couple satisfaction after meeting through that site. The study revealed these findings:

- Over 90 percent of eHarmony couples had marriage quality scores that were above average, when compared to couples who had begun their relationships elsewhere.

- eHarmony couples were more than twice as likely to be in highly successful marriages than non-eHarmony couples.

- Not only were eHarmony couples 35 percent more likely than other married couples to report that they enjoy spending time together, but also they were nearly twice as likely to report that their marriages are "extremely happy" or better versus other recently married couples.[2]

On the surface, it appears that eHarmony provides the platform to connect well-matched people for long-term relationship success. It may lead us to believe that compatibility is the key to that success. It seems undeniable that a couple matched by compatibility in numerous areas will have a higher chance of having a successful marriage. However, isn't it also likely that emotionally healthy people are being matched with equally emotionally healthy people and those who don't score so high aren't included in the pool? If this is the case, then it may be a great place for emotionally healthy people to meet others with a healthy operating system.

eHarmony's brilliance is not only in providing a forum for emotionally healthy people with similar interests, characteristics, and other compatibilities to meet each other, but also in reducing the risk that an emotional 10 (healthy operating system) will end up with an emotional 2 (Complicated OS). If you're proactive enough to care about searching for a com

---

[2]Available at http://www.eharmony.com/

patible partner, then using a method such as eHarmony's might be of value.

It should be noted that the study provided no data on the eHarmony failure rate for comparison. Also, no independent studies of eHarmony's methods or success rates have been published.[3]

If compatibility is the answer, or at least a part of the answer for those with a healthy operating system, what about the person with the Complicated OS? Is compatibility the answer for them? If not, why not?

Connect . . . Disconnect

Even though most single people are looking for that special someone with whom to spend their lives, the person with the Complicated OS is desperately seeking to be in a relationship. Why? Because their operating system tells them they feel empty without it—a hole that can only be filled by another person.

Because of the chronic feeling of emptiness, he seeks relationships to fill that void. He is governed by rules that tell him that to *feel* good or to *feel* complete and whole, he must be **connected** with another person or persons, whether it be a romantic partner, children, parents, or maybe even a good friend. The need to be connected with another human being and stay connected is a driving force that is unmatched in its intensity and power. It is most pertinent in the romantic relationship although it can extend to other relationships. Our focus for purposes of this book is the ro-

---

[3]This book is not an endorsement for eHarmony. It is only a commentary on their methodology, which is consistent with one of the themes of this book.

mantic relationship because it is the most likely and natural place for it to appear.

Conversely, the rules that govern the healthy operating system tell her to take time getting to know prospective romantic partners to look for signs of trouble. She doesn't feel *incomplete* without a romantic partner. This does not mean she isn't desirous of having a relationship, being married, and living happily ever after; she just doesn't *need* to be in a relationship to feel whole nor does she need to rush into exclusivity.

When the Complicated OS does not feel connected, anxiety sets in, making it hard to breathe. Relationships that come to an end are quickly replaced with a new relationship because the time and space between them puts the Complicated OS in panic mode. I've often seen someone with a Complicated OS quickly end a relationship that up to that point had been a life-or-death *must stay together* relationship, as soon as they connect with a new person. I've seen others who consciously establish a new relationship, making sure a solid connection is established before letting the old one go.

It happens a lot, but these two stories stand out in my mind:

In the first case, *the girl met a cute guy to whom she quickly attached herself. They had an immediate spark and intense attraction. Over their three-year relationship, he rarely took her out in public and never introduced her as his girlfriend to his friends or family. She thought about him all day while at work and waited for his call every evening, hoping he would invite her to spend time together on the weekend. From an outside perspective, it was easy to see that she was willing to settle for his crumbs and that he was stringing her along to suit his own needs. For her, it was enough and she* *was willing to do anything to stay with him, even forgiving him for cheating on her. Her friends and family were entirely confused by this strange logic and tried to talk her into ending the relationship. What they didn't understand was the relationship provided her with just enough air to keep her breathing, that it filled an empty place . . . just enough. When she didn't hear from him, she began to feel disconnected (anxiety, panic), so she would check in with him or modify her behavior and actions in some way with the hope of reeling him back in—to once again feel connected. Then, after three years, she broke up with him without warning, something that seemed impossible up to that point. It turns out that she'd unexpectedly met someone new who gave her a little more air than the old boyfriend. The new guy gave her a lot of attention and wasn't embarrassed to be seen with her in public—in other words, she had full girlfriend status. Without the new air supply, ending the first relationship would have never happened, but having a new air source prevented that uncomfortable feeling.*

__In the second case,__ a woman who had been married for more than twenty years had long been tired of her marriage and badly wanted a divorce, but no matter how many times she tried leaving, she just couldn't do it. Eventually, she used her significant financial means and winning personality to set up a new life in a different city while maintaining her marriage. She established a temporary home, friendships, jobs, potential romantic partners, and anything else in the new setting that would give her enough connection (air) to disconnect from her husband and file for divorce. To the average outsider, it simply seemed that she was a woman who was going through a hard time. To the person with an understanding of the complicated OS, it was obvious to see that her life was like a set of air hoses—each one providing some air (connection) to hopefully replace the air hose to her husband. Sadly, as often is the case, the new relation-

ships did not work out either and she was back to feeling miserable in her marriage.

The Complicated OS wants to feel connected. Think about how you would feel if your oxygen mask were removed at thirty thousand feet. Wouldn't you do anything you could to get oxygen? The fear of taking your last breath weighing heavily, you would do anything within the realm of possibility to get that oxygen.

The person with the Complicated OS is desperately seeking *connection*. In addition, there's another significant and important difference between healthy and complicated: this person doesn't even know they're starving for connection. To them, it is natural and normal to feel a strong desire to be connected, and they have no idea that it's not that way with everyone. Disconnection creates anxiety, which drives the need to reduce and eliminate that anxiety. Their operating system drives them to connect, which, of course, means doing anything and everything to connect, even if it's with the wrong person.

It all begins to make sense when we understand the Complicated OS. She puts her best face forward when meeting new people, especially potential romantic partners. Driven by the need to eliminate the feeling of emptiness, she may be overly sweet, caring, charming, flirtatious or even seductive—all to connect with another human being who will make her feel whole.

This is the *bait*, albeit unknowingly and unwittingly initiated by her. It's normal to her. She is programmed this way. Not evil, not bad, not strategically manipulative. Just needing to connect. This is about brain development and a way of relating of which she's not aware. She's sucking you in because she needs air. (There are people who are strategically manipulative in relationships; that's not who we're talking about here).

Complicated OS connecting happens in a variety of ways:
- overt flirting
- touching the arm, shoulder, hand during the first conversation
- overly complimentary of everything about you
- overly agreeable
- overly available
- overly adaptable
- overly selfless
- overly helpful
- overly helpless

Others say or do anything to show they are more compatible with you, the prospective partner, than anyone in the world, while some are overly sensual, sexual, or flirtatious from the beginning. This desire to connect brings out amazing qualities in the complicated person that *hook* us into wanting to know this interesting person with whom we have an immediate spark.

Usually, we feel a strong connection right from the beginning and we're drawn in because it's nice to be appreciated and to have someone pay attention to us. If we're in dating and looking mode, we are probably also in lonely mode, so it feels nice to be flirted with and given special attention. We might even be vulnerable. Or flattered, which makes us vulnerable.

You may have heard the term *chameleon* in reference to someone like this. He might adapt his likes/dislikes, interests, schedule, and even his geographic location to connect with another person. A woman dating a guy who likes surfing suddenly has an interest in everything to do with surfing, although she previously despised getting in the ocean. A man who previously had no interest in riding horses quickly develops an interest in riding after he begins dating a new person. Most people want to show interest in their potential partner's interests, but the complicated person adapts too quickly and easily.

Unfortunately, this seeming adaptability is housed within the same person whose operating system is rigid and inflexible after the relationship is formed (more on that in the next chapter).

This dynamic was interesting to observe on a reality dating show in which a bachelor is presented with a slew of female candidates from which he chooses a potential wife. When it came down to the final few candidates, the finalists were flown to the bachelor's hometown—a very small town in the Midwest with just a few hundred people. Upon arrival, one candidate, the only one with whom the bachelor had an immediate and intense spark right from the beginning (she did a lot of hugging and non-sexual touching with the bachelor and other candidates), didn't look too pleased at the prospect of living in the country outside of a town with nothing to do. She was from a large city in a warm climate and the most unlikely candidate to adapt to a solitary country lifestyle without restaurants, beaches, and all that city life has to offer. However, by the time the short hometown visit was over, just a few hours, she made an amazing turn-around and stated that she could happily live there forever.

The other candidates accused her of being a manipulative liar and told the bachelor as much. They couldn't comprehend that she was not being intentionally manipulative.

Looking at it through the Complicated OS lens, her switch makes perfect sense. Although her initial reaction to the small town was less than favorable—a normal response— it flipped the *disconnect* switch on because it meant that marrying the bachelor (connecting) would be off the table. That acknowledgment led to discomfort, anxiety, and made it hard to breathe. What did she need to do to start the flow of oxygen again? To survive? She had to adapt. Her brain quickly formulated a plan to make her feel *connected*, to get the oxygen flowing again so she could breathe. The powerful force of the complicated OS overrode logic choices. The other contestants turned against her and she melted in tears, truly hurt, wounded, and confused by their "attacks." To her, the adaptation was natural and came from a pure place. To her, it was *true love.* Her quick switch wasn't a strategy nor was she cognizant of it.

This is not to say that other people in a similar situation would not choose to move to a small town for love. The difference is that a person with a healthy operating system will typically consider and weigh their options over time instead of quickly and impulsively making major life decisions.

Summary

A powerful need to connect with another or at least temporarily feel connected with another human being is the primary force in the Complicated Operating System. It unconsciously works in the background, directing the person to go to great lengths to find a person with whom to forge a lasting connection. It tells the person that another human being can fill a chronic emptiness, that another person can satisfactorily provide every want and need. It's driving the relationship, but it's driving it with unconscious, false intensions. The complicated OS tricks the person into thinking that connection is the answer; however, the honeymoon doesn't last long. It quickly (for most) or eventually (for many) evaporates; a switch occurs and the relationship turns into a chaotic mess. In Chapter 4, we'll uncover the second part of the complicated OS—the confusing, self-sabotaging behavior and conflict patterns after the relationship is formed.

CHAPTER 4

The Complicated Operating System: Behavior within the Relationship

The Complicated OS craves *connection*, as we learned in Chapter 3, but within a matter of time it also unknowingly *sabotages* that very connection. The desperate need to be in a romantic relationship is only half of the Complicated OS equation; the other half is everything that happens after the relationship is formed.

Beyond Connection

Now you're in a committed relationship and the mind-blowing intensity that drew you in has since turned into an unpredictable rollercoaster of extreme emotions and events. In the beginning you were likely drawn to the excitement of those extreme, intense emotions, but now they've turned into a nightmare.

- Will she come home in a good mood or sour mood?
- Will I get blamed for everything again?
- Will he embarrass me or throw me under the bus in front of my family and friends?
- Will we be up all night going around in endless illogical arguments?
- Can I trust that she won't vandalize my car or cut the legs off of my jeans?

- Will I always feel like I have to be responsible for his happiness and for fulfilling his every need?

- Am I going to encounter another war later if I don't answer my phone now?

- What will get broken? Will I get scratched or hit again?

- Will she threaten to or actually jump out of a moving car?

These are shocking for obvious reasons, especially in comparison to your experience in other relationships, but it's become your reality. It's difficult to reconcile that a nice, sweet person can also be so vicious and out-of-control, and equally difficult to comprehend that the switch from good to bad can happen in the blink of an eye. A pleasant conversation that instantly turns to rage.

While such extreme upsets seem unpredictable, you may have learned to predict that they *will* happen, but you just don't know *when*. A big question mark hovers over your relationship that causes you to be on guard most of the time.

What is behind this erratic, unpredictable, uncomfortable, chaotic behavior? Why would anyone change from sweet, caring, and loving to manipulative, raging, controlling, or hopeless? Is the behavior actually intentional? Can't they see that their behavior is extreme and outside the norm? Why would anyone want to be in such a miserable relationship? Remember, these are the type of relationships that seem unfathomable unless you've personally been in one.

Most of us will never be able to truly make sense of this kind of behavior or see how we can save a love relationship with such a person. Despite a thorough search, we simply cannot find a road map for dealing with this person.

We read book after book trying to understand but never fully grasping why someone would behave in such an unruly way and how we can possibly restore the relationship to health. There are many great relationship books on the market filled with useful strategies for managing, salvaging, and healing relationships. But, by and large, these books are written for the ordinary relationship struggles that most people go through; they don't address the deeper needs of the complicated relationship—an entirely different and deeper category of difficult relationships.

Gaining an understanding of the second half of the Complicated OS will help make sense of the extreme behavior and chaos in which you live. The second half is:

1) creating chaos that sabotages the relationship (connection), and

2) protecting the connection as if life itself depends on it.

Sabotaging the Connection

Think back to the need for connection and its purpose of filling the emptiness; the much-needed air to alleviate anxiety. The Complicated OS brain feels that along with connection comes a cocoon of safety and security. Many describe it as a safe harbor, a place they can finally relax and feel safe and secure. They can breathe. It's easy to believe and logical to assume that a romantic connection would satisfy the emptiness. However, the opposite is true. Lasting satisfaction is usually short-lived and it's not long before emptiness and a *threat* of feeling disconnected creeps in. In other words, *connecting* provides temporary relief from emptiness, but not a cure.

Why does the Complicated OS sabotage the very thing

that would satisfy it? Again, it doesn't make sense without looking through the Complicated OS lens. Remember the emptiness that drove your partner into a relationship in the first place? It comes from *within* your partner. It cannot be cured or fixed by a relationship, even though that's what makes it feel temporarily okay.

So now you're together in the relationship and you're beginning to see some red flags that weren't there in the beginning. She may want you to be available to talk 24/7 or place expectations on you to fulfill her every need. These expectations are all consuming and overly demanding for you: "I want you to listen to ME. I want you to understand ME. I want you to want to know ME. I need you to stop the bleeding. I need you to ALWAYS be there for ME. I need you to be the bandage for my pain."

The bandage analogy is common among people with a Complicated OS. I've heard many people say they feel like they're bleeding (emotionally) and it's their partner's responsibility to apply a bandage to stop the bleed. When the partner can't stop the bleed, the fight escalates, the Complicated OS feels like it's still under threat. And your partner simply feels bad.

Because the flaws in her operating system come from within, they cannot be fixed by merely being in a relationship with you. The need for connection hasn't gone away. Eventually, the Complicated OS begins to feel uncomfortable and empty when it doesn't have something to worry about, which causes it to create issues, pick fights, or fire up some type of drama. It creates disharmony out of the blue and out of nothing. Hey, a fight is connection.

An argument can feel terrible for you but for your partner, it solves a problem. She will take connection in whatever form she can get it. Remind yourself that she isn't consciously conspiring to make your life miserable. She is driven by the Complicated OS.

And you'd better believe that the connection will be protected like Fort Knox.

Protect the Connect

You might be starting to catch on to the importance of the connection. It is the central figure to the story, the key to understanding what's going on in your life. You now know that it drives the need to be in a relationship and then, still unsatisfied, creates chaos to continue feeling connected. Next, it's critical to understand that the almighty connection must be and will be protected at any cost. Recall that for your partner, feeling disconnected feels like a loss of oxygen, so it makes sense that they will do everything humanly possible to protect the connection.

When he feels connected, he feels safe. He doesn't feel anxious or afraid. But when he feels disconnected, whether the feeling is valid to you or not, his brain will fully perform its protection duties with rapid-fire speed. (Remember, your partner doesn't know this is going on behind the scenes. The only thing he feels is anxiety and fear of disconnection that propels him to do whatever it takes to eliminate the fear).

If you've wondered why your partner is so jealous of your friendships, your relationships with family, or even casual acquaintances or strangers, this is why.

His system is constantly on the alert for threats to the connection. Typically it's your relationships with other people that, in his mind, provide a threatening feeling to the connection. Physical separation can also trigger the feeling, and in some, it can happen even while you're together.

People as Threats

The Complicated OS can decipher between *safe* and *unsafe* people. It will feel threatened by what it perceives to be unsafe people. Your partner's brain picks up on this unconsciously. She experiences sudden fear that produces anxiety—she suddenly feels horrible and it spills out on you. Safe people can be trusted; unsafe people cannot be trusted.

A few examples of things you do that can trigger your partner:

- Spending time on the phone talking, texting, or on social media
- Paying attention to anyone other than him or her at a dinner party, in a conversation, or at work
- Not including him or her in the conversation
- Your relationship with your parents, your children (mostly in cases with stepchildren), siblings, or other relatives
- Planning a trip that includes other people, without including him or her in the planning

Your partner may have demanded that you choose between other people and him or her, insisting that they are bad and out to sabotage your relationship.

Let's consider the case of a man whose mother is upset because his wife ignores her and rarely allows her access to her grandkids. His wife has insisted that his mother interferes too much in their lives, she's not good to the kids, and she's mean and condescending. This may be the case in some relationships, but in the Complicated OS, his wife feels a threat to her relationship (connection) with her husband. It's intolerable, so her brain needs to eliminate the threat. The mother-in-law's presence or even the thought of her presence creates anxiety in the wife. She doesn't want to feel anxious. She did nothing herself to cause the anxiety, so she believes that the feeling comes from the mother-in-law. In the meantime, the husband stammers around not knowing what to do and tries to make peace where he can. Unfortunately, without an understanding of the need to "protect the connect," he may make it worse or perpetuate it.

I was involved in a situation once that gave me a clear view of "protect the connect." On a Friday evening, after a conference I'd helped organize in another state was over, I was ready to call a taxi to pick me up and take me to the airport to fly home. One of my colleagues who lived in that city offered to drop me at the airport, which I gratefully accepted. His phone rang once we were in the car. It was his ex-wife demanding that he come to her home right away to pick up their kids, even though she had agreed to switch weekends with him so that he could run the conference the rest of the weekend. Hoping to avoid her wrath, he said he would be right over to pick them up. It was on the way to the airport. I had some background information about their "high-conflict" divorce and instinctively knew my presence in the car wouldn't go well. I asked him to drop me at a convenience store or gas station near her home, and then pick me up again after the kids were in the car. It sounds sneaky, but I strongly suspected that my presence would pose a threat to her and I wanted to avoid any trauma to their kids and to myself.

Instead, he said he would get the kids while I stayed in the car. All was well until I was startled by a loud banging on the window right next to me. She'd come around the back of the car and there she was, yelling at me to roll the window down, wanting to know who I was, what I was doing in the car, that I had no business being around her kids! Remember, she was a complete stranger to me. My heart rate increased, I felt under attack, and was barely able to mutter anything intelligible back to her or figure out how to roll the window down. She came at me with rapid-fire accusations and statements. My colleague was trying to get his young children in the car. They were scared and uncomfortable, although this was probably not a rare event for them. So, what happened here? I strongly suspect that her Complicated OS started to feel threatened earlier in the week when told about the conference. It was out of the norm and could possibly mean new people and attention away from her—a threat to the connection. She had nothing else to do that weekend, so there was no reason to shuttle the kids back to their dad other than to throw a wrench in his ability to spend time with other people. She was the one to end the marriage but she needed to protect the connection. How did she know there was someone in the car? I can't say she sensed it, although I suspect she might have. She could have looked out the window and saw me in the car. Regardless, it activated her radar detector for threats to her connection. You can believe I breathed a sigh of relief when I was eventually delivered to the airport.

Geographical Threats

The above example was event-driven, but we see this displayed in everyday life with physical separation. Many people describe daily separations when leaving for work as the most difficult part of their day. Instead of a normal send-off greeting with "have a great day" from their partner, tearful or angry statements or accusations are made. Could it be that you feel badly because you know your partner will feel sadness the rest of the day? One distraught person frequently had to change shirts before heading out the door in the mornings because his wife would scratch his back to the point of bleeding. This is an extreme example, but it's not rare.

A client once described the lengths to which he had to go to satisfy his girlfriend's demands. As a frequent business traveler, he had to fly once or twice each month. Before the plane took off, he had to surreptitiously take a picture of the people on either side of him on the plane, and then text them to his girlfriend. Why? To prove he wasn't sitting by a hot girl.

Threats When You're Together

Threats can also happen when you are spending time together. These can occur in the form of jealousies over text messaging or being on Facebook while sitting together watching television. Being together in the same room enjoying an activity together would seem enough to keep threats at bay, but a phone call that comes in during that time, time spent texting, or anything on the phone can be felt as a threat.

Turning your back to your partner while in bed can be felt as a threat, as can walking away in the middle of a perfectly normal conversation, even if it's just to get a glass of water across the room.

You simply need to understand that anything that takes attention away from your partner may be felt as a threat. It's not because your partner is intentionally being mean or wanting to make your life miserable. As hard as it is to fully take this in, it's very real. It seems irrational, but it's not. It all makes sense within the Complicated OS. Help for dealing with these situations are in the second half of this book.

Summary

The Complicated OS is different from a healthy OS because:

1) Being connected in a relationship is a driving life force

2) Once connected, the fear (threat) of being (or feeling) disconnected becomes the driving life force

I hope that these chapters have given you the understanding that your partner has a different operating system when it comes to relationships; that it centers around the need for and threats to the connection to you; that it will protect that connection no matter what. Sadly, if you don't understand that your partner is not intentionally sabotaging the relationship and making your life hell, you will become depressed, hide, walk on eggshells, fight, or grow increasingly frustrated, helpless, and confused. You've been applying the wrong strategies, which keeps your relationship in chaos.

You will find hope and help in the coming chapters.

CHAPTER 5

The Complicated OS Brain
in the Complicated Relationship

N ow that we have a clearer behind-the scenes picture
of why your relationship is in the state it's in, you may
wonder how the brain developed this way and how
it impacts your relationship.

How does the Relationship Operating System develop?

In the 2012 movie *The Angel's Share*, a new baby was born
to first-time parents who were young and unprepared for
parenthood. Before the hospital allowed the couple to take
the baby home, a nurse explained that a baby is born with
just half of its brain, and the other half is up to the parents—
up to them.

This was not exactly scientific, but a poignant piece of advice intended to help new parents understand just how
critical they are in their child's brain development in those
first few years of life. Our parenting in those first years ultimately shapes and strongly influences our children's future
relationship success or failure.

The relationship brain begins developing before we're born
with something called temperament—the way we approach

and interact with those around us. You might think of it as each person's unique individual style; we can be easy and flexible, active and feisty, or slow to warm and cautious (Vanderbilt University, 2011).

After we're born, those critical first developmental years design the rules of our Relationship OS. The recipe for a healthy relationship operating system is supported by decades of research about child development. Children need protection, nurturance, and love the first few years of life—most importantly during the first five years. They need a secure attachment (meaning a good trust and protection relationship between a child and parent/caregiver). This is fundamental to building a healthy relationship operating system. Good future relationships depend to a great extent on these factors, as well as having good examples and role models for resolving conflict.

The presence or absence of trauma plays a large role in future relationship health, especially if the trauma has never been resolved (meaning we "stuff it" and avoid thinking about it or do not allow ourselves to feel the uncomfortable feelings that come with it). Childhood traumas like abuse, particularly sexual abuse, that remain unresolved or untreated affect our future relationships. Other traumas, like parental conflict, play a part as well. Study after study shows trauma causes a great impact on brain development and future relationship success. We even have brain imaging technology now that reveals size differences in certain parts of the brain for people who experienced abuse or other traumas as children.

To be clear, not everyone who experiences trauma or abuse ends up with relationship difficulties. Often, interventions occur that help a child recover and move past trauma or they develop resiliency in some other way, whether it be a relationship with a grandparent, another adult, or some other type of help.

Essentially, it is these ingredients that form our Relationship OS. The more untreated trauma, the more likely we are to have a Complicated Operating System, which naturally leads to difficult romantic relationships down the road. All of this underscores the critical nature of good parenting and protecting children from abuse of all kinds—neglect, trauma, and parental conflict.

As we develop, our brain grows quickly during those first years of life. Just as our bodies need good nutrition and exercise, the brain needs good input to make it healthy, too. We need all parts of our brain to have the chance to develop normally so it can have optimal performance. To get a better understanding of this, it will help to know about basic brain function in human relationships.

Right or Left Brain or Both

We know more about the brain now than at any other time in history. Neuroscientists have made significant strides in understanding how the brain works, its many disorders and malfunctions, its genius, how it develops, and what is required to develop a healthy brain. Pioneers in the field like Antonio D'amasio, Daniel Goleman, and others have opened even more windows that give us insight into the brain's influence on human interaction, emotions, and relationships.

Most people know if they are more right-brained or left-brained. Do you think of yourself as a right-brain or left-brain person? We typically associate left-brain people with engineers, lawyers, or accountants; and right-brain people with artists, musicians, and other creative and artistic careers. While this is mostly spot-on, these same right and left hemispheres go far beyond guiding our career choices and what we like or don't like to do with our time. They also dictate, in concert with other brain parts, how we handle relationships, and most importantly, how we handle conflict in relationships.

What we now know is that the interaction between the left "logic" brain and the right "relationship" brain, combined with "jobs" performed by other parts of the brain such as the amygdala, hippocampus, and corpus callosum guide our human interactions.

The Logic, Problem-Solving Rules Left-Brain:

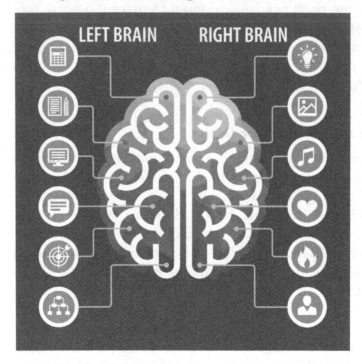

Left Logic Brain

The left hemisphere has a specific job to do. It is generally known to be responsible for helping us solve problems through a logical process of analyzing and planning. If you're applying rationale to a problem, it's a left-brain activity. The left-brain is conscious—that is, we know we are thinking.

Both hemispheres are assigned a set of emotions, and positive emotions like being calm, peaceful, and content are anchored in our left-brain.

Various researchers and authors assign different names to the left-brain when it comes to conflict resolution and relationships, such as: the logic brain, the rules brain, and the problem-solving brain. Our left-brain, which operates more slowly than the right-brain, one thought at a time, helps us have moderate behaviors and emotions and to think of many solutions or options to problems. The left-brain uses systematic processes in a methodical way to help us find solutions to problems by coming up with multiple options and analyzing them one at a time.

I think of my husband as an ultimate left-brain problem-solving kind of guy. His responses to my questions come painstakingly slow, at least in my opinion, but over time I've learned that his left-brain is hard at work to first understand the problem, and then develop and analyze options before producing the long-awaited answer (it's truly just a matter of seconds rather than minutes). It's easy to picture punching some numbers into the old-style computers that filled a room back in the 1960s and then pushing the "calculate" button. Then, we settle in during the calculation phase and wait for the printout. Interestingly, the output is spot-on, as he's known to be an excellent problem-solver.

Right Relationship Brain

The right hemisphere also has a specific job. It is generally known to be responsible for helping us with relationships, and it works unconsciously, or without us even knowing that it is working on our behalf. The right-brain is known to be associated with creativity, facial recognition, gut instinct, and observing relationships. Where the left-brain is associated with positive emotions, the right-brain is associated with negative emotions like hurt, fear, and anger. When I mention this in workshops, people are usually surprised. It seems we assume that the creative side would relate to positive emotions and the logic side would be more rigid and negative. However, the opposite is true.

The right-brain is called our relationship brain or defensive brain. It works very quickly and is responsible for helping us assess situations for danger and to get us out of harm's way in those times.

Right and Left Joined by the Bridge (Corpus Callosum)

It makes good sense that to make good, well-rounded decisions we need both hemispheres to communicate quickly back and forth with each other. The more they work together, the better decisions we make. The fast, defensive relationship brain checks in with the slower logical problem-solving brain. Back-and-forth, back-and-forth.

While we may identify more with one hemisphere than the other (like my husband being a strong lefty), in reality we use and need both hemispheres.

Between the hemispheres is a critical part of the brain called the corpus callosum that serves as the "bridge" to transport information between the two hemispheres. You might think of it as the communication highway. Researchers tell us that we want a thick bridge because it has many more neural pathways to transport information. We've also learned that more flow between the hemispheres is better as it provides the benefit of the best of both hemispheres. Essentially, it integrates information transferred between the hemispheres.

A study released in 2013 by the Oxford publication *Brain: The Journal of Neurology* (Weiwei Men, Dean Falk, Tao Sun, Weibo Chen, Jianqi Li, Dazhi Yin, Lili Zang and Mingxia Fan., 2014), reported that Albert Einstein's corpus callosum was thicker than most others, likely lending to his extraordinary genius (along with other anomalies like a robust pre-frontal cortex where executive functioning occurs). In layman's terms, his "bridge" was more like a freeway with many levels and lots of lanes.

The Almighty Amygdala & Pre-Frontal Cortex

Our brains come equipped with a right amygdala and left amygdala. In relationships, we focus on the right amygdala. Neuroscientists tell us it's approximately the size and shape of an almond.

To help us understand better, let's use this analogy. The right amygdala works somewhat like Wi-Fi. It's invisible. It's like having a personal 24/7 watchman on guard to alert us to danger, all done without us even knowing about it. As we interact with each other, our right amygdala is assessing the other person's facial expressions, body language, and tone of voice. However, we don't know it is always working hard on our behalf to protect us. It's stealth.

When the amygdala is alerted to a potential threat, whether real or not, it fires up in less than a second and immediately shuts down the bridge from Right Relationship brain over to the Left Logic brain. It disables the Left Logic brain temporarily.

I like to think of it as a radar detector; searching for threats and preparing us to respond. When it detects danger, it shuts down the bridge from Left Logic brain to Right Relationship brain; sends cortisol through our body which tightens our muscles and prepares us to protect ourselves with fast action.

Think of the movie *Top Gun*. Tom Cruise, in his role as a fighter pilot, uses the plane's radar system to scan the skies for incoming threats. Once he sees a blip on the screen, he must immediately analyze the threat and respond. Does that blip represent an enemy or not? If it's an enemy, he pulls the trigger launching the weapon to destroy the threat. If he determines that it's just a flock of birds, he doesn't pull the trigger. He's using left-brain logic to make the assessment.

Why does his right amygdala not close his bridge to the left-brain logic? Because another part of his brain, the prefrontal cortex, steps in to override that response, enabling him to access his left logic brain. That's its job.

Putting it All Together in the Complicated Relationship

What do Tom Cruise and all these different brain parts have to do with the Complicated Operating System and complicated relationships?

To be clear, I am not a neuroscientist and although I've spent years reading about the brain in relation to human relationships, I am not an expert on the brain and some of what I discuss in this book is debated between neuroscientists and those in the psychology profession. Debate swirls about which parts of the brain are responsible for certain activities.

What I will attempt to do here is relate what I've learned in my own research and what I've gleaned from others who know much more about the brain than I; most particularly, from my co-founder at High Conflict Institute, Bill Eddy, whose fascination with the workings of the brain in relation to conflict is legendary (a listing of his publications along with many others about the brain can be located in the Resources section).

In the Complicated OS, the brain developed in such a way that creates a strong desire to be connected with another human being. It feels lonely, anxious and afraid when disconnected and it demands to be connected in order to feel okay, to feel relief. The only way to satisfy the disconnect is to connect, so the Complicated OS drives the person to do their utmost best to "sell" themselves as someone you'd want to be in a relationship with. The brain says, "the only way to satisfy this bad feeling is to connect." The desire is so strong that the person will usually adapt in just about any way to facilitate attraction and connection. The brain lets them think that as soon as they are connected to the other person, the bad feelings will go away and be replaced with positive feelings. They want to make the relationship permanent, usually speedily. The brain tricks the person into believing that another human being can solve the problem, not understanding that it's an underlying issue that cannot be solved or resolved by another person. The feeling of connection lasts for a while, but eventually the same old feelings of emptiness and disconnect set in, particularly when that other human being cannot be available 24/7 or meet our needs in every way.

So, the Complicated OS goes back to work in an attempt to feel connected. It picks fights and does whatever it can to feel connected. You engage or run from the negative interaction—both of which further their feeling of being disconnected.

When you engage, you use words, logic, and persuasion to calm your partner or get her to "see" a logical perspective; however, this only serves to only agitate her more. Why? Because, at this point in time, she only has access to her right hemisphere where negative emotions are stored, and she's reacting without the benefit of access to her left logic brain. It's *illogical* for you to use *logic* when she has no access, or limited access, to her *logic* left-brain.

When you run, the fear of feeling disconnected, or abandoned, is triggered. Your partner may run after you, fly into a rage, fall into sobs, or even throw or hit something (or someone).

You as the partner do everything humanly possible to be available 24/7, only to painfully discover that satisfying that ever-present need to connect is impossible.

The Complicated OS continues feeling dissatisfied and needs more connection. You try, but can never satisfy the problem, so to the Complicated OS feels like it's all the partner's fault. "You don't tell me you love me enough. You don't want to spend enough time with me. You don't want to get to know me in the way I need you to get to know me. You don't care. You don't see how hard this is for me. You don't understand that you are the cause of my pain. If only you would pay attention to me, to my needs, to who I really am. If only you would care enough to put my needs ahead of your own for once."

Your options may seem limited. If you stay, you lose. If you run, you lose. There are other options, which we'll talk about in the second half of this book. In the meantime, you're exhausted.

CHAPTER 6

Wrapping Your Head Around Your New Reality

Are you breathing a sigh of relief with this new insight? Or maybe you are still skeptical about the notion that the behavior is not intentional?

Wrapping your head around the reality that your partner's behavior is not intentional is critical if you want to meet the goal of reducing stress, pain, fear, anxiety, and chaos. More importantly, it will help you possibly save your relationship and create a better and happier life for both of you.

Accepting the Reality

Why is it so important to accept the reality that you are in a relationship with someone who is not only different from your expectation, but whose behavior is not intentional? Here's why: because if you do not accept it and cement this reality into your thinking, you will be stuck in the trap of using the wrong strategies in your interactions. Your relationship will continue to be chaotic and won't have a good chance at succeeding long-term.

Full acceptance of the reality is tricky and you may find yourself going back and forth wondering if it is bad behavior or a Complicated OS. The person you see in front of you may have a job, friends, or hobbies, which makes him or her seem "normal" or at least capable of behaving better in your relationship. You may be asking yourself why it is that they can keep a job, act normal in front of other people, and keep a house clean, yet they wreak havoc when it comes to your relationship.

The truth is that anyone who has to deal with this truly does not *want* to behave this way. The behavior is painful for them, not only in the moment but all day, everyday.

What we fail to comprehend is that the person causing this chaos has no idea that they create conflict or that they handle relationships and conflict differently from other people. Think about it. We think the way we think. We adapt to various things over time but without the awareness that we have different operating systems. We think that we all share one type of system to varying degrees.

This is probably the most difficult piece of information to fully accept, but it's also the most critical, for once you have it, you are elevated to the level of understanding required to deal with it. It automatically instills empathy for this person who struggles, but doesn't know it. Not only do they *not* know they have a different operating system, they likely think you're the one with the problem.

Bad Behavior or Fear-Driven?

In some cases, the switch from great relationship to chaotic mess is sudden—right after the wedding or moving in together—while in others it may have happened more gradually over a period of months or years. When it is sudden, it is shocking. In many cases, it can appear as though the person has had a psychotic break or nervous breakdown. In the old days, they might have been sent away for a while or straight to a mental hospital. It's obvious that the extreme behaviors are outside the norm and you either accept it and adjust or end the relationship. Many people stay in the relationship for a long time without an understanding of their partner's behavior. Most do not survive although some do as long as the other adapts to an extreme degree.

With the sudden onset of chaos, accepting the reality that the behavior is not intentional may be a little easier than in cases where the switch occurs over a longer period of time. You may see the rapid behavior change as an intentional bait and switch; "acting" nice just to "trap" you into marriage, and once the marriage happens the "real" person appears. This is a frequent misconception. We don't realize that the fear-based thinking is the driving force.

Is it someone behaving badly—just a rotten person—or is it someone with a Complicated OS? When it happens this quickly, it may seem obvious that something is outside the norm and beyond their control. In relationships where the demise happened gradually over time, there may have been a good relationship for years. When it turns chaotic, we grow accustomed to the behavior as it gradually changes, even if we don't like it or feel comfortable dealing with it. In this case, it may be more difficult to accept that your partner's behavior is not intentional and the wounds may be so deep that the source of chaos just doesn't matter anymore.

A World of Opposites

Keep in mind the Complicated OS from the previous chapters. This operating system affects **relationships** although it is fair to say that this is not one size fits all. Some people who have this kind of relationship operating system also have problems keeping a job, maintaining friendships or relationships with family members, and other issues. Others, frequently referred to as "high functioning," are affected primarily in the romantic relationship.

You will need to remind yourself that just because your partner functions well in other areas of life does not mean they have the ability to function well in your relationship. The operating system in play is the opposite of what you expect it to be.

If it helps, take a piece of paper and draw a box in it with a line down the middle. Inside the left box, write "RELATIONSHIPS", and "EVERYTHING ELSE" in the right box. Every time you think your partner is just being difficult on purpose, think about this graphic to remind yourself that he or she may have the ability to function okay in other areas of life, but relationships are more difficult.

Relationships	Everything Else

As you change your strategies, you will begin to see that your partner's behaviors are *opposite* of what you would expect. The strategies you've applied are for someone with a Healthy OS, which is why they haven't worked well for you. Instead, you will discover that doing the opposite of what you *feel* like doing, are *used* to doing, and *want* to do, will have the best chance of working for both of you.

You may need to remind yourself about the Complicated OS more frequently in the beginning, but over time it will become part of your regular thinking. Be prepared that it may take a long time for this new thinking to become engrained and natural.

Empathy

Empathy is the action of or natural instinct to put yourself in someone else's shoes to understand how they feel. It's hard to do this with your partner because your way of thinking is opposite of his or hers. You may be required to dig deep to generate empathy, especially when you are being attacked or just plain worn down from always being on alert. If you find empathy difficult to generate, try these tips:

- simply accept instead of trying to understand
- think of the good and happy parts of your partner
- think of the bad behavior as temporary
- imagine him or her as a wounded person who needs help, even though hostility may be coming from him or her
- challenge yourself to rise to the challenge of helping make both lives better.

The wiring of his or her operating system began long before you came into his or her life. You did not cause it, but now you are involved in it and you have to accept that your relationship is different. There are no delusions that this will be an easy endeavor, but with patience, practice, discipline, and love, it can become easier over time as your partner begins to trust you and understand him or herself.

Grieving

With this new knowledge comes relief, but grief often accompanies it. You're relieved because someone understands what you're going through and has a name for it, but saddened because your dreams and plans to have a happy, "normal" relationship or marriage are gone. It's a loss that needs to be acknowledged, grieved, and accepted.

You don't want to get stuck in grief so be aware that grieving the loss of a perceived *normal* relationship is *normal* and let yourself go through the stages of grieving whether that be denial, anger, bargaining. Eventually you need acceptance to complete the grieving stages.

Deciding

Once you've grieved the loss of your desired relationship, you can move on to deciding if you can commit to:

- understanding and accepting your partner's Complicated OS
- adjusting your expectations
- becoming disciplined enough to truly help your partner

No one says it is easy, but I believe there is hope because I've seen it happen many times. A successful outcome is possible although it does not mean that every relationship can be saved. Your partner also has a part in success or failure—it doesn't all depend on your actions although your actions will have a significant impact on his or her success. This is one way to think about it: you may be blessed with a healthy operating system, which means you are not operating in a fear-based mode. Your partner does not have this same ability, so you will need to adapt what you do because your partner truly does not have the ability to adapt his or her own behavior. At least not yet. You have to make the first move.

The impact of empathy cannot be over-stated here. The mere act of accepting your partner's operating system naturally and holistically builds empathy. True, honest empathy is not a strategy but it can result from a strategy to understand.

Taking Care of Yourself

You're not in an easy relationship. It's likely already taken a toll on either your mental well-being, physical health, finances, or other relationships. You may have lost yourself over the course of this relationship, so it's important to assess your emotional and physical health before going forward.

You will be able to deal with this relationship if you're taking care of yourself. Do you take time for yourself daily to do something you like to do, without worrying about getting in trouble? Do you take a walk or do some other physical exercise at least once a day?

These and other forms of self-care are vital to your next steps. Your best you is incredibly important at this stage.

Do You Have What It Takes to Stay?

Do you believe that your partner has a Complicated OS?

Can you stand firm and develop boundaries even if you

would rather hide?

Do you truly have empathy for him or her?

Can you weather the extremes that come with this behavior, especially in the beginning?

Do you have the courage to challenge yourself to be honest no matter what?

Take some time to consider these questions and come back to them occasionally to remind yourself that your partner operates differently in relationships and you need to adapt your actions to help the person you love. With acceptance, you lay the foundation to function differently in your relationship and are now ready to learn new ways to manage it.

Summary

Accepting that your partner's difficult behavior is *unintentional* is key to stabilizing your relationship. A large part of the solution is accepting that he or she does not choose to be this way, nor is there an awareness of it. Grieve the loss if you need to; remind yourself often to have empathy; and commit to taking care of yourself so you can move forward with confidence.

PART II

Creating a New Environment
to Manage the Relationship

CHAPTER 7

Establish a Threat-Reduced Environment

N ow that you have a better understanding of your relationship, it's time to start taking steps to stabilize it.
The rest of this book provides an instructional manu-
al for dealing with a complicated relationship and shifting it
into one of balance.

The goal of Part One was to introduce the Complicated Operating System to help you see your partner's behavior in
a new light. A window should now be open that deepens
your understanding and empathy.

In Part Two, you have the opportunity to replace the old
way of doing things with new strategies that are designed
to give you the tools to reduce chaos and bring stability and
peace into your life . . . and save your relationship.

Some changes can be immediately implemented, but others
take longer because they require practice and experimentation.
Understand now that you will have failures—some strategies
will work better than others—and you won't respond appropri-
ately to your partner every time. Sometimes the Complicated
OS takes us by surprise and in those times we revert back to
the way we are used to reacting. But don't despair or give up.
With practice, you will find it easier to respond to your partner
in ways that foster connection and reduce conflict, and you will

be motivated by your partner's successes and the peace that begins imbuing your relationship.

The coming chapters focus on:

1) establishing a new, threat-reduced environment (what you can do from a big picture perspective)

2) learning to manage the Complicated OS instead of letting it manage you.

Deciding to Seek Outside Help or Not

Before we delve into how to establish a threat-reduced environment, it is vital to state once again that these are the most difficult of difficult relationships; they can range from moderately to extremely difficult. Violence or abuse of some kind is often present in the complicated relationship. You may think you're helping your partner by putting up with it, but the opposite is true. Allowing it perpetuates it. Fighting back puts both of you at risk of harm, not to mention it's completely unhealthy for the relationship.

The tips provided in this book will be most helpful in the moderately complicated relationship, but they may also assist people in more difficult scenarios. If your situation is critical and out-of-control, seek counseling or help from another professional outside source, especially if abuse or any type of violence is involved.

If you need immediate help, call 9-1-1, or contact an abuse hotline. See the Resource section on page 157 for more referral information. Below is an assessment designed to help you determine if you should seek outside assistance.

SEEKING OUTSIDE HELP ASSESSMENT

1) _____ Your partner throws things at you, hits or scratches you, or otherwise physically harms you.

2) _____ You have hit, scratched, or otherwise physically harmed your partner in retaliation.

3) _____ You feel out-of-control or nearly out-of-control, or you've overreacted in a violent way during arguments with your partner.

4) _____ Your partner harms himself or herself or threatens to.

If you answered yes to any of these questions, consider seeking outside help. Again, look on page 157 for more resources.

There are other kinds of abuse, including verbal, emotional, and others. It's never okay to accept abuse of any kind. You may be able to calm some of the outbursts of abuse, both physical and verbal, by learning new strategies in the rest of this book. However, some people need in-depth outside assistance from a licensed mental health professional who is skilled in relationship issues and trauma treatment.

This book is not intended to replace or serve as a substitute for counseling. It is intended to help you gain an understanding of why your partner behaves the way he or she does in relationships and offer strategies and skills you can use in your interactions. You may need to seek counseling together or separately.

Why You Need to Establish a Threat-Reduced Environment

Your partner's system is in a constant state of alert, scanning for potential threats. It wants to feel safe, connected, and positive, and you can be a big help to change from a threat environment to a safer environment.

Think back to what you learned about the Complicated OS. The person with it operates in a threat-based environment, either feeling disconnected when you're gone or constantly scanning the people around him for potential threats. He fears *feeling* disconnected from you. His brain is hyper-vigilant to that threat—whether it seems real and logical to you or not. In his perception, the threat of disconnect is so intense and strong that he is driven to find any way to regain connection, which may seem anything but logical. His reaction won't come across in the way you would ex-pect and here's why: the feeling of disconnect stems from the fight-or-flight alarm activated in his brain. While it's dif-ficult—nearly impossible—to fully comprehend how intense and powerful this feeling is, let's try.

Think about the *thing* you fear the most. Maybe it's spiders, snakes, heights, or _____ (insert your worst fear). For me, it's being in a vehicle on a highway with black ice—a thin layer of ice on a highway that is difficult to see and so slick that the vehicle can easily spin out of control. I'm terrified of it, especially if I'm not the one behind the wheel. My heart rate increases, muscles tighten, and all of the cells in my body feel like they're on fire. The fear is so powerful that I will do whatever it takes to eliminate that feeling, which sometimes entails getting that car pulled off the side of the road as quickly as possible! I'm none too pleasant to whoever happens to be driving, especially if they don't understand my fear. It's powerful, it's intense, and it propels me to take control.

You've probably experienced something similar with your own fear. Your reaction might seem extreme and irrational to others, but makes perfect sense in your own mind.

What do we do? We take control of the situation. We avoid snakes, frogs, heights, or black ice. Your partner can't avoid his fear; it's his operating system. He can't avoid people.

Now think about operating in this fear-based mode as a way of life (remembering it's not by choice). It's not that he is in a fear state all of the time; rather, his brain is constantly looking for threats to his connection with you (whether that's from an outside source or from you) and when his brain perceives threats, it triggers fear. On and off. Up and down. The threat feeling can lead to anything from mild annoyance and upset to red-hot anger that bubbles out without a filter.

How Does Your Partner Feel Your Relationship Is Being Threatened?

First, let's talk about the kind of things someone with a Complicated OS may view as threatening to your relationship. Some of those threats are real—that is, they do somehow take away from your ability to focus on and connect with your partner—and others are threats only in the person's perception.

For the Complicated OS, a real threat includes anyone or anything that puts your relationship in danger—it somehow takes away from your close involvement and connection. This threat can be a friend, parent, child, or stepchild; it could even be a random person. For example, both of you know that it's natural for you to have a relationship with your mother, but for your partner, time spent or attention given to your mother can nonetheless feel like a threat to your relationship. It's hard to imagine, but it is very real to your partner. You may feel like you have to hide other relationships and live in fear about what will happen when you take the time to see your mother or whoever it is that causes your partner to feel neglected.

Unlike these types of real threats, which are tangible and somewhat easy to sense or see, perceived threats are unconscious and unseen for the complicated person. And for us, the partners, they are the threats that take us completely by surprise.

As we've discussed, when you're together in person, the right amygdala continuously searches your face, voice, and body for potential threats and then goes into action trying to eliminate or destroy them. It automatically fires off "missiles" to destroy the threat without waiting for input from the part of the brain that regulates emotions. Was the threat real? Not to you. However, without your partner even knowing what's happening, the situation *feels* very real and powerful to her. And all of it launches in less than a second.

What does this look like? Say, for example, that you are happily going about your business without a care in the world on a perfectly fine Saturday afternoon. You suddenly find yourself involved in a huge fight with your partner that spins out of control. You have no idea why or how it started. The incident happened so fast it made your head spin and you are confident that you did nothing to cause it.

It's confusing and scary, especially when you haven't experienced it before. Even if you've been together for a long time and are no longer scared when such situations occur, you might still be confused. Consider this scenario, which demonstrates how it usually happens:

Leah and Blaine were out with Leah's work friends on a Friday night. It was Blaine's first time meeting them. Everyone was having a good time and Blaine tried joining in the conversation with a joke or two. Suddenly, he stood up, knocking his chair back, and stormed out of the restaurant. Nothing or no one could stop him—he was on a mission.

The group sat in stunned silence, completely in shock, having no idea what had just happened. Embarrassed, Leah had nothing to offer in explanation, so she stayed at the table thinking she would just give Blaine a few minutes to cool off. After twenty minutes she realized he still hadn't returned so she went to look for him. He was sitting on the curb by the car with his head buried in his hands. When Leah asked what happened, he responded by shrugging his shoulders at first and then began using words, hurling accusations that she didn't care about him, love him, respect him, or want him. That she had ignored him, didn't include him in the conversation; she made him feel like a loser and unwelcome in the group. With increasing volume and intensity, he stated that he ALWAYS had to explain this over and over to her but she NEVER remembered and obviously didn't CARE about him or that he felt BAD!

Leah, with an incredulous look on her face and hands on her hips, stated that he was being ridiculous! Of course she cared about him, but couldn't he see that everyone was just having a good time? He responded, repeating what he'd already said, but with more intensity and frustration. Now he was standing up. Leah's frustration also grew, her voice became louder, and she kept trying to reason with him and give what seemed like logical explanations to her. They continued arguing for another minute or two until Blaine yelled that he'd had enough and took off running. Leah went back inside to explain to her friends that she *needed to leave. She gathered her purse, hopped in their car, and found him walking a mile or two away.*

What really happened? Blaine usually had a hard time fitting in with new people but he tried his best. These were Leah's friends with whom she had a long history and established friendship and they had a lot of inside jokes and stories about work that didn't include him. As the evening wore on, he began to feel increasingly disconnected from Leah as the stories and laughter continued. At one point, Leah turned her chair so that the back of it was faced away from him—yet another disconnect. One disconnect built upon the next, which caused his anxiety to correspondingly increase. The final straw for him came when he tried joining the conversation with a joke that fell flat. Leah gave him a sideways glance with a look that his amygdala *read* as embarrassment. Blaine's brain, already in a heightened state of anxiety because it felt left out, translated this as a threat, fired off in less than a second, and filled him with immense anxiety that sent him flying out of his chair.

If you could have asked him in the moment what had happened, he would have explained that he was being ignored and excluded by the group and that Leah had been rude and condescending.

Leah would have reported that she was trying to include him but it was difficult because he didn't work with them, so he wasn't privy to their inside jokes. She would have said she was not being rude or condescending, nor were her friends ignoring him.

Outside, Leah responded with logic and explanations. Her face (incredulous) and body (hands on hips) told him he was being ridiculous. Her tone of voice (loud and somewhat defensive) told him he was bad and wrong.

A response that came across calmly and with kindness would have put out the fire in his brain. He was stuck in right-brain negative emotions and couldn't access the logic left brain.

Threats come in many forms. Your understanding of this threat system will transform how you approach and handle conflict in your relationship. Let's look at a few examples.

Potential threat:
Spending time on your phone, device, or computer on social media; talking on the phone; instant messaging; emailing.

Scenario: You are on your phone or other device while watching television together. You think you can kill two birds with one stone as you multitask: spending time with your partner watching your favorite shows, and taking care of a few emails from work. Your wife asks a question or two about your day, the kids, anything. You ask her to hold on for a minute while you finish your email. She's obviously agitated but you think she can wait for a bit. Then your phone rings from someone you sponsor in AA, which happens often. This person needs assistance and you never turn down a request for help; plus, you've committed to being available to this person anytime. Your wife blows up at you and now you're in turmoil again.

Why it feels like a threat: Attention shifts away from your partner, causing her to feel disconnected. You likely see it as jealousy or control, but the core is about disconnection. In this scenario, each instance of feeling ignored escalated her feeling of disconnect.

Solutions:

- Develop a specific time of day to check your email, use social media, and perform other Internet-related tasks. At the same time, and even more important, plan, implement, and stick to a specific daily routine to spend time with your partner. Set aside this time for just the two of you to discuss the day, schedule the coming days or weeks, talk about future plans, etc. For some it may work best to schedule this in the morning, even if it's just a brief time to have coffee together before work, and then a longer period together in the evening after work. The key is to give undivided, undistracted attention to your partner. Make it a non-negotiable. What does that mean? Ignoring the phone, device, and computer.

- Decide together what time of day works best for both of you to meet. Develop your own list of possible times and ask her to provide a list of options also. Do not do all the option-generating. It's *imperative* that the complicated OS be given problem-solving tasks such a coming up with ideas and options. You may feel like avoiding what can be a painfully laborious task, but pull out a pen and paper and get both of you writing lists of options, and then choose the day and time that works best for both of you. Put it on the calendar and stick to it. This builds structure and trust in your relationship.

In some cases, phone calls are unavoidable. Decide what is important to you and make a list of priorities. But I urge you to adhere to and make your special daily time together a non-negotiable time of not taking calls, answering emails, etc.

Help for you: You should not feel like you have to, nor should you, hide phone calls and communication with others in your life. This is about keeping your partner's threat level down. If you spend a lot of time talking with others, whether it be through instant messaging, phone, Facebook, or other social media venues, your partner will feel more disconnected from you and, consequently, her threat level will likely go up. You might want to examine your priorities and make some slight adjustments. You can and must have friendships and relationships with other people, but try to put your relationship first, without sacrificing your other relationships. It's okay to have balance in your life.

Potential threat: Excluding your loved one from planning, especially when it involves others.

Scenario: You're on a weeklong ski vacation with two other couples. Throughout the week you gather several times to plan where the group will go for dinner, where you will ski, and other details. This is a group of strong personalities, except for your husband. They made all the decisions without realizing they excluded your husband the entire time. He maintains his composure within the group but seems grumpy and agitated. On the drive home, he is very upset and complains that you and the others excluded him all weekend. You have no clue what he's talking about or why he would feel this way since he was present every time plans were discussed. It goes round and round until he's yelling and eventually tells you that he feels so terrible he wants to jump out of the car while it's moving.

Why it feels like a threat: The Complicated OS wants nothing more than to feel connected and included. When it feels left out or unwelcome, it feels disconnected, causing it to feel out of control and on fire.

Solutions:

- Whenever plans are being made, remind yourself of your partner's need to feel connected. Make a point to include him in the conversation, ask his opinion, and consider his input along with everyone else's. It's not that he's needy or controlling. He just needs to feel worthy of being included. As you include him, the threat of disconnect will dissipate for him.

- Suggest to the group that each person take a different day/night to plan an activity/dinner, and make sure your partner is assigned to one or at least given the opportunity to volunteer or not.

Help for you: This should be an easy scenario to handle.

Dealing with Anger and Hostility

When the amygdala is triggered and the pre-frontal cortex doesn't stop bad behaviors from spewing forth, the person acts with anger and hostility, quite the opposite of what you would expect from someone who desperately wants to connect with you. While it would seem logical for your partner to behave nicely in order to connect with you, that's not how the Complicated OS works. It does the opposite of what you expect. We have to think back to the complicated brain. It wants to connect with you, and when it feels the threat of disconnect, it reacts immediately with force.

To reduce the conflict and calm the situation, you must do your own bait and switch by countering with a response opposite of what you are used to doing, what you want to do, and what you feel like doing. A lot of times you will feel anger and you'll want to fight (explain or defend) or flee the situation. But, if you want to stabilize your relationship, you have to practice doing the opposite of what you feel like doing. When your partner is angry or triggered, instead of responding with words, explanations, defenses, anger, or laughter, flip your own switch into *connecting mode* and later into *shifting strategy*. We will talk about connecting and shifting in the following chapters.

Seeing Red

Some people with a Complicated OS describe anger as so intense they actually see red. If you haven't experienced anything like this yourself, it's impossible to truly understand it. Suffice it to say, it's one of the most powerful feelings a person can ever have. What happens with that intense feeling? Because the Complicated OS doesn't do a great job regulating emotion, it doesn't stop the anger from pouring out—and it may (or likely will) be directed at you. This anger can come in many forms, some that you may be able to deal with and some that should never be tolerated:

- yelling
- cursing outside her norm (saying the F word or calling you horrible names)
- throwing whatever is already in his hand or any nearby object
- slamming doors
- stomping around with clenched fists
- hitting walls, throwing chairs

- driving recklessly (rage driving)
- raging on Facebook or other social media (posting comments that vindictive and harmful to your reputation)
- running away quickly
- banging her head on the wall
- threatening to jump or actually jumping out of a moving car
- hitting you
- scratching you

This behavior can be confusing and illogical to you and it may make you angry and want to stay and fight, or scared and want to hide or run. Most people don't understand what has happened when they see and experience a hostile, seething, angry person before them who spews out verbal vomit or violence of any kind.

Our natural first response to our partner's anger and hostility is to defend ourselves. There is nothing wrong with that; in fact, you must protect yourself. Abuse is never acceptable. I can't emphasize this enough. If you are in this type of situation, safely remove yourself and seek outside assistance. Your loved one needs help that is greater than you can provide or that you should be required to bear.

If you've been dealing with verbal, emotional, or physical abuse already, you may have grown used to it or find that you're numb. Or you might fight back—a strategy that is not healthy and will backfire. Regardless, any violence or abuse is a sign of a toxic situation that needs changing. You may think that you are protecting your partner by putting up with it, excusing it, doing your best to avoid it, or fighting against it. **Quite the opposite is true—you are actually en-**

abling the behavior. You then have a part in keeping your partner, your relationship, and you sick. If you're in a violent situation, seek outside help and keep yourself safe.

Final Thoughts

You will need to dig deep to find empathy for your loved one at times, but trying to understand the pain your partner is feeling will ultimately benefit your relationship. Remember, your loved one is feeling extraordinarily powerful and intense emotions. The experience is exhausting and debilitating for your partner (and for you). This is why it can be so helpful for you to practice skills and strategies that reduce the threats your partner experiences in the environment (although you won't be able to anticipate every threat).

You will create unending value by developing and maintaining a threat-reduced environment. At times, you may feel like it's not fair that you have to take steps that others don't have to do in their relationships. When you feel this way, be sure to take some time for yourself to refresh your batteries. This is particularly important when you are beginning to use your new skills. You will have to draw on your reserves of compassion, empathy, and love for your partner. Remind yourself that your partner's behavior is not about you, it's not intentional, and you can walk beside your partner to help him or her navigate life a little better.

CHAPTER 8

Get Unhooked

The next step is to understand your role in the chaos. This piece of the puzzle is **critical** because it can help you prevent or contain arguments and rage. Your reactions and responses impact every interaction with your partner in a helpful or harmful way. At this stage you are probably aware of what *does* and *does not* work and know much more about what *doesn't* work than what *does*.

This chapter will help you understand what works and reduce what doesn't.

Conflict Response in the Moment

Do you know how you respond to conflict and how you are impacted when involved in conflict with others, especially with your partner? While everyone reacts differently, we generally fall into one of three categories: fighter, flyer, or freezer.

Think about a group situation where several people are gathered around a table for a meeting to discuss a project they've worked on for many months. Toward the end, one group members raises a question about something she thinks they missed—something that was vital to successful completion of the project. Another member, with an irritated tone to her voice, responds that they didn't miss anything and just need to get the project finished. They go back and forth a few times, but it seemed innocuous and not unlike other discussions within the group. However, there was a strange vibe in the air. Everyone went quiet except one person who looked the question-raiser directly in the eyes and said that he understood what she was trying to say. The leader then steps in saying they would discuss it next time and then called the meeting to a close.

What happened? No one yelled, made accusations, or personal attacks. The room just *feels* tense; like the air can be cut with a knife. Everyone senses a negative 'vibe'. Everyone had a reaction.

Why is everyone around the table affected? Just like the person with the Complicated OS, everyone has a threat detector – that built-in defense shield with an alarm system (amygdala). The difference is that the defense system of the Complicated OS is hyper-alert—in other words, it's an over-achiever. Once that person's amygdala senses a threat, the person instantly feels anxiety (increased heart rate, fear, intense urge to fight or run) and a look of anger or fear may cross their face or eyes, which activates everyone else's amygdalas. Now, everyone around the table has a conflict response. Some want to enter the conversation; some want to flee from the room; and some are frozen in place. Fight, flight or freeze.

What is happening? The brain does its job by going into rapid-fire action increasing the heart rate, sending chemicals through our blood stream to tighten our muscles and prepare us for fast action and shutting down access to the left logic "problem-solving" brain. The right "defensive" brain, which controls fight, flight and freeze, steps up to defend us. We feel a strong urge to fight or run away. The good news for most of us is that other parts of the brain step in to regulate these emotions and stop us from fighting or running.

Around the table, people responded this way:

two people kept quiet (flyers or possibly freezers)

one joined in the argument (fighter)

one nervously looked around for an exit (flyer/freezer)

one closed his eyes and willed himself to stay in the moment and help the upset person calm down (flyer with good conflict override skills)

The argument could have gone on and on until they either resolved it or someone (most likely the Complicated OS person) fled the room. Many conflicts end this way because we fail to understand and recognize there is a Complicated OS involved. However, in this example the group member who intervened was able to stabilize the situation by using good connecting skills.

This example was used to illustrate that relationships are happening even when we don't know they are and everything seems calm and normal. Hopefully it will help you understand why you respond the way you do.

Are You a Fighter, Flyer or Freezer?

Ready to find out if you're a fighter, flyer, or freezer? This test will help you understand your conflict style.

During a heated argument with your partner, you:

A. stay in the argument trying to persuade your partner to accept your point-of-view and logic

B. seek the fastest exit, wanting to flee as quickly as possible

C. seek the fastest exit, wanting to flee as quickly as possible but instead you feel tongue-tied and frozen in place

If you answered (A), you tend to be more of a *fighter*. This doesn't necessarily mean you like to pick fights or slug someone in the jaw; rather, your natural tendency is to stick with a discussion or argument using logic to prove your point. You do not feel like running from the situation.

If you answered (B), you tend to be most comfortable in turtle mode (also known as ostrich mode); in other words, like a turtle, you prefer to get under your shell or like an ostrich, bury your head in the sand when you sense conflict. You want to get away from the discussion or argument as quickly as possible because uncomfortable anxiety has already set in.

If you answered (C), you also tend to be like a turtle or ostrich but the anxiety is so high during times of stress in a discussion or argument, you tend to simply freeze. You prefer to be invisible or maybe even evaporate from the room.

All humans will react in one of these three ways. There is no wrong response. You are what you are. These are natural instincts and they are just how we are made; however, once you learn your conflict style, you can better understand why you react the way you do to your partner. Then, you can begin practicing new ways of handling conflict, overriding your old reactions and, instead, respond.

Respond, Not React

It is important to know your natural conflict response style so you can learn to *respond* rather than *react*. This is helpful in any relationship but critical in the *complicated* relationship because your partner's emotions are sudden and intense, catching you off guard and putting your stress system on high alert. Remember, the fight or flight response fires off in less than a second. Not only do you not know *what* happened, you don't even know that something *has* happened until you feel like you're under attack.

Your heart rate increases, muscles tighten and you suddenly want to either engage in discussion, problem-solve, defend yourself, run from the room, hide under a table or say something but find that you can't. These are intense, powerful feelings. Sometimes we can override or wait out these intense waves of anxiety but other times we get *hooked*.

Getting Hooked

What does it mean to get "hooked"? It is the moment when fight, flight or freeze is activated and we succumb to it. We don't override it. It's the "critical moment" in conversation with your loved one when you feel like fighting or fleeing. You forget about the Complicated OS and using a different strategy, and instead you defend yourself, try to use logic and explanation, or do anything you can to leave the room. It all depends on your conflict style.

For example, your partner just accused you of spending too much time at your friend's house. You think it's a ridiculous accusation so you respond with an explanation. Your partner obviously doesn't accept your answer and levels more accusations against you, and you keep responding. The baited hook was thrown, you took the bait, and now you're hooked. What the Complicated OS wants is connection, and what you're doing is defending *being* disconnected. There is nothing wrong with going to your friend's house, but it's made your partner *feel* the threats of being disconnected. You naturally want to respond with logic and explanation to defend your actions, but what's really needed is *connection*.

For others, as soon as you feel the familiar anxiety, you want to get out of the room and away from the situation. You're hooked.

This simple test will help you know if you are susceptible to getting hooked.

Are You Hooked?

In discussions or arguments with your partner, do you:

1. find yourself using logic that doesn't get you any-where and seems to only make things worse?
2. find yourself shutting down?
3. ever, or often, overreacted, far outside your norm, during discussions or arguments with your partner? For example, yelling when you're not usually a "yell-er"; cursing; kicking or hitting something.

If you answered "yes" to any of these, you've been hooked, and it probably didn't feel very good when you realized it.

It's vital to not get hooked by your partner. Remember, it's his brain that's doing something very automatic. It wants to connect, so it will tempt you, bait you, or seduce you in some way into connecting. It's already frustrated and stuck in negative right brain emotions. It's begging you to con-nect, to pour water on the raging fire in his right brain.

You might assume it would be lovely, cordial and polite to get what it wants, but it's not. Instead, it comes out with anger, raised voice, or some other hostility. Then, not know-ing any better, because you're used to defaulting to your way of doing things and because your amygdala is probably triggered by the anger coming toward you either by tone of voice, body language, words or facial expression, you get hooked and stuck in the endless, spinning illogical argument.

How to Get Unhooked

Awareness is king. You must commit to adopting a new and constant awareness of the Complicated OS. If it helps, think of it like learning of a loved one's cancer diagnosis. You would be open to doing many things differently once you were aware of the diagnosis—change of diet; doctor visits; chemotherapy; among other changes. The difference is that a cancer patient knows they have cancer; your partner does not know he has a Complicated OS; but, you do, and now you know that you have to do things differently.

Listen with the Complicated OS translator. Remind yourself that what she's saying is different from what she really wants. When she says, "I want you to l-i-s-t-e-n t-o m-e!", what she's really saying is, "I feel awful right now and the only thing that can make it better is for you to connect with me right now."

Respond like a fireman trying to calm a child who's just been rescued from a burning building. In other words, respond with calmness and confidence. Think about your body language, tone of voice and facial expression. Say things like, "Hey, it's a bummer to see that you're upset about this. I'm here to help you figure it out." Or, "Are you okay?" "Can I help you?" "Awww, let's figure this out together."

How a Fighter Gets Hooked and Unhooked

The Scenario

Kari was okay with her husband's work routine, but she would get upset when Tyler was late coming home in the evenings, especially if he did not call or text to let her know. By the time he walked in the door, even if he was just thirty minutes behind schedule, the inevitable stone cold silence greeted him. He tried asking how her day was and what was on the menu for dinner, but she continued ignoring him until he quit asking her. This prompted Kari to start questioning him about being late, and especially why he hadn't called. Tyler, not realizing how upset Kari was and had been for a while, responded with an explanation for his tardiness and went to change his clothes and get comfortable. He hadn't stopped to think that she was anything more than slightly miffed. When he turned to walk away toward the bedroom, Kari followed him demanding that he pay attention to her and answer her questions – all with increasing intensity and volume.

Tyler kept trying to explain but quickly got confused about what was happening. He didn't notice his increased heart rate because it was happening so quickly. This back-and-forth went on and on until he lost his cool and yelled back. Kari ran from the room, slamming the door behind her and cried herself to sleep on the couch.

How Tyler the Fighter Got Hooked

Tyler got hooked because his natural inclination was to explain what had happened without realizing a war in Kari's brain had started forty-five minutes before he walked in the door. He wasn't wrong in staying, but he erred in not switching gears and communication methods. He tried to explain his actions and inactions and defend himself, forgetting to switch gears and use his Complicated OS skills.

What Kari was Experiencing

Kari became increasingly upset waiting for Tyler to come home. She did not plan to be upset or even want to be upset. She just felt upset. Unknown to her, she began to feel disconnected which made her feel uncomfortable and anxious. She did not have conscious knowledge of it – she just felt bad and because she hadn't done anything to cause herself to feel bad. Not that she was logically thinking this through necessarily, this is what her system was processing.

By the time Tyler came home, her system was on red alert and even though the one thing she wanted more than anything was to connect with him, she did not know how to communicate that to him or tell him what she needed, mostly because she was trapped in defensive right brain emotions, lacking access to logic left brain problem-solving. In her upset state, she threw a few hooks to start the conversation (connect), to which he responded with explanations and defenses. His response had to first process through her defensive brain, but explanations and defenses during stress and upset only fire up the right brain's defenses and close the bridge to the logic, problem-solving left brain.

She was stuck in anger and hostility, maybe even rage but she did not know how to stop it or that it even needed stopping. She felt very clear, logical and justified. She could cut every one of his words with her verbal sword, which, in Tyler's view, didn't raise red flags because she sounded so logical. This inadvertently 'tricked' him into explanations and defending. She tried explaining over and over why she was upset over his lateness and that he didn't truly care about her, about upsetting her, about her need for him to be responsible, how bad he made her feel, and many other trying complaints. But he just didn't get it. Everything he said didn't make sense to her or solve the problem. In fact, it only escalated her anger as she repeatedly tried to get him to understand.

It didn't take long for the expletives with the volume cranked up to start coming out. When she was so overwhelmed with emotion, she fled, slammed the door and fell apart in sobs. She wanted Tyler to comfort her and felt that only his comfort and attention could relieve her distress. Instead, Tyler left her alone thinking that she wanted space and time to calm down.

What Tyler Should Have Done for a Better Outcome

Even though Tyler had experienced this scenario many times in the past, he was in a good mood after a regular day at the office and was still thinking about work when he walked in the door, not expecting a problem at home. His natural logic, problem-solving mode extended from his work world to home leading him to apply problem-solving to the complicated situation. His problem-solving and explanation translated to 'fight' in Kari's brain. His explanations only escalated her anger and distress.

Eventually he got frustrated because his problem-solving had no impact and then he began to feel attacked after trying his best to address the situation. He did not feel like fighting or want to fight, but he continued talking to her left logic brain, not remembering that she wasn't ready for that yet. She needed connection, not logic.

Instead, he should have tried this course of action:

First: Change his approach with Kari. He should remind himself to be aware that he cannot use the same approach with her that he does with other people. He must adapt his approach to the entire relationship, thinking globally of the strategy that works for the complicated person. It requires thought and discipline but over time it will become more natural.

Second: Remind himself that he needs to **connect first** and use **logic and problem-solving later** or not at all. He should always remember that he's like a fireman whose job is to put out the fire first.

Ideally, in this situation he would let Kari know he was running late. That small action would have helped her feel less disconnected and the right defensive brain calmer. When he walked in the door, he could go directly to her with open arms and a warm smile, thanking her for being patient with him on these late work nights. He must be genuine and remember that during these times of upset and stress, even when she is spewing verbal vomit, it is important to take the time to address the situation. He should be aware of these valuable tools to use in upset moments:

- Switch from problem-solving to stabilizing
- Remind himself that she feels fear and disconnect – it's not about being late
- Connect with her by paying attention, using a calm tone of voice, and body language that shows he is interested.
- Stay with her, continuing to use words and body language during cool down

It takes an investment of time and discipline but the payoff for both Kari and Tyler is huge. Instead of intense, destructive fights that leave both of them feeling terrible and that could go on for hours or days, the conflict can be reduced to minutes. Often times, the mere act of connecting causes the original complaint to disappear, never to be discussed.

Understanding your conflict style and adapting your approach to conflict will have a powerful impact on your relationship. Connect first.

CHAPTER 9

Relationship Management: Connecting

From this point forward, remind yourself that you won't be doing things the old way any longer. Going forward you are using a new strategy—one that is specifically designed for communicating with the Complicated OS. Mark the day on your calendar as a new start to the Complicated OS strategy; find some physical object that you adopt as your visible reminder that you're doing things differently. It could be a rock, a piece of jewelry, or anything that will help you remember to do things differently. It's a new beginning!

One of the hardest things you likely dealing with endless arguments, defensiveness, accusations, personal attacks, and your partner seeing himself as a victim. You might have several days without disruption, but even then you usually feel like you're walking on eggshells or need to fly low under the radar so you don't get fanged, blamed, or accused.

This chapter is about daily relationship management. Because your partner lacks the ability to successfully manage his or her role in the relationship, you have to do it for both of you.

You should see some improvements early on, but don't have high expectations for quick changes, and don't assume you will "cure" or change your partner. Her relationship management skills have been developing throughout her life. Your goal is to contain the behavior to better manage the relationship. You're taking a step back, looking at her through the Complicated OS lens so you can make sense of what's happening, changing your reactions to responses, and managing the relationship.

Let's start with learning a new way to manage your relationship in everyday life.

Your New Strategy

Your new strategy is as simple as these four valuable actions: *connecting, shifting, honesty, and consequences.* This chapter focuses on connecting. The following chapters focus on the others.

▶ **CONNECTING**
   Use *connection* to calm the relationship right brain (negative emotions).

SHIFTING
   Use *shifting* to activate the logic left brain (positive emotions).

HONESTY
   Use *honesty* to honor yourself and provide boundaries for your partner.

CONSEQUENCES
   Allow *consequences* to help your partner learn.

Connecting

Always keep in mind that your partner operates in a fear-based, threat-based system. The more your partner feels connected, the less fear and anxiety she feels, and the more your lives improve. When he feels disconnected, arguments begin. He just needs to feel connected.

Although you can't be completely responsible for her happiness or for her to feel connected all of the time, there is benefit to both of you if you make this a part of your new operating system. If you take on the impossible task of solving all of her problems are being responsible for her happiness will keep you in an unhealthy mode and keep your relationship sick.

Connecting is about managing. When you sense or see some fear-based behavior, inject some connection into her system. Here are some ways to connect:

▶ **With Words**

- "I can understand that could be difficult for you. It would be for most people."
- "I went through something similar myself."
- "That really stinks!"
- "I feel bad that you're not feeling good about this."
- "It's hard to be in a position like that"
- "I love you."
- "You're a strong person. You're smart. You're capable."
- "You can do this!"
- "I believe you have the moxie to get through this."
- "Sometimes life just doesn't seem quite fair, does it."
- "Let's think about this."
- "I'll give you my full attention right now."

- "I love you. I want to give this my full attention. I have to go to work right now, so let's set aside time tonight to talk more about this. Should we do that before dinner or after dinner? What time do you suggest? What will work for you?" (in all likelihood, the event may go away simply because you've given it attention now)

- "Did I tell you that you look pretty/handsome today?"

The Goal
The goal of your words is to give empathy.
Empathy equals connection.
Connection puts out the fire in the right brain.

What to Avoid
Avoid judging or criticizing.
Avoid making digs or zingers, even if you feel like it. They will backfire.

What you're Feeling
You may be triggered and feel like saying something:
- sarcastic
- mean
- condescending

Or you may not be triggered but use:
- logic
- explanations
- words to defend yourself

Override your feelings (do the opposite of what you feel like doing), and remember to use *connecting* language.

Override your pattern of using logic and explanations. Instead, us *connecting* language.

Important note: these are two of the hardest changes to make because you're used to going with your feelings and/or you are used to using logic and explanations. All of us want to defend ourselves, especially when under attack. Practice this a lot. Get in the habit each morning of reminding yourself to respond differently.

The result of using explanations and logic is an ever-increasing frustration in you, because they're not working. Your explanations and logic are going into her right relationship brain where they get stuck. They don't reach the logic left brain because the bridge between is closed for business at the moment. You're wasting your breath and time, not to mention how illogical it is, using logic on the non-logic side of your partner's brain.

▶ **With Tone of Voice**

- Use a soft tone of voice
- Use a calm tone of voice
- Use a firm tone of voice

The Goal

The goal of using a soft, calm voice is to avoid further triggering your partner.

The brain is soothed by a soft, calm voice; it's aggravated by a loud or angry voice.

A calm brain turns into a *thinking* brain instead of a *feeling* brain.

What to Avoid

Avoid using a voice with:

- contempt
- anger
- accusation

- interrupting (your partner will feel like he is not important – this is a biggie)
- disbelief
- loud volume
- criticism

What You're Feeling
You may feel overwhelming:

- anger
- frustration
- disbelief

Override those feelings (do the opposite of what you feel like doing and are used to doing) and tell yourself to use a calm, soft, non-judgmental tone of voice.

Important note: Tone of voice is mentioned more often as a trigger by those with a Complicated OS than some of the other triggers. Remind yourself that your partner is not choosing to be "sensitive" to tone of voice. It's her amygdala that is picking up on it without her even knowing it.

▶ **With Facial Expressions**

- Look your partner directly in the eyes – not in an aggressive way; just a way that says "I'm paying attention to you."
- Use a look of concern.
- Smile
- A look of contemplation.

The Goal
The goal of your facial expressions is to show empathy.
Empathy is connecting.
Connecting puts the fire out.

The goal is the same as above with tone of voice—his amygdala is hard at work analyzing your facial expressions. Remind yourself that his amygdala works harder than yours at detecting potential threats. That means you need to work harder on using facial expressions that express empathy and attention.

What to Avoid

Avoid:

- Hateful looks
- Looks that convey you think she is crazy
- Hostility
- An incredulous look
- Disgust
- Rolling your eyes
- Sneering
- Glaring

What You're Feeling

You may be triggered, frustrated, annoyed, disgusted, or feel attacked. Remember, it's not about you. This is about the Complicated OS.

Override your temptation to stare her down, or, most tempting, roll your eyes, or anything that will fan the flames.

▶ **With Body Language**

- Turn your body toward your partner in a non-threatening way (it shows attention)
- Tilt your head to one side or the other (similar to how a dog looks at you when it wants to understand what you're saying)
- Lean forward (to show attention, but not in an aggressive way)

- Stop what you're doing and sit down to show you're going to give this your time and attention

The Goal
Body language shows attention.
Attention equals empathy.
Empathy equals connection.

What to Avoid
Avoid:

- Smacking your forehead with your hand
- Shaking your head in disbelief or frustration
- Banging your head (even in a faking way) on a wall, table, etc.
- Giving the finger
- Putting your hands on your hips, especially with your feet in a wide stance
- Putting your hands up (in the way you would if a police officer told you to put your hands up)
- Shaking your fist
- Walking away, especially while talking or hurling insults
- Turning your back to your partner
- Grabbing your phone to look at emails, texts, etc.
- Throwing or hitting something

What You're Feeling
You may feel so frustrated that you can't think of anything else to do. You may feel stuck, or even out of control. You might think your body language isn't giving a message, but it actually sends powerful messages.

Override your feeling to run away or stay and fight, and concentrate on using body language to calm your partner's brain. Tell yourself to use this as an opportunity to practice your skills.

When you can connect, do so. Picture her having a hard time breathing with no access to an oxygen mask or air hose; or a right brain that's on fire but with no water to cool it down. **You** are the only one with an oxygen mask. You are the only with a pitcher of water or a garden hose to put out the fire. She truly does not have the ability to help herself when she's in this state. Eventually, the goal is for your partner to get help through proven therapies (see the Resource section), that will help him or her develop skills to regulate emotions and stay calm. In the meantime, you are in the best position to

Make it a Part of Life

Try not to be overwhelmed thinking that this seems impossible. Instead, see it as a kindness you can extend to the person with whom you are in love. If you have failures, forgive yourself and try again next time. You are not perfect. You may overreact sometimes and raise your voice, throw your hands up in despair, walk away, turn your back or, God forbid, roll your eyes. You will notice that you don't meet your goals this way. So, try again next time.

Use your brain to tell yourself to switch from your regular relating mode to the mode that works with the Complicated OS, and that starts with connecting.

CHAPTER 10

Relationship Management: Shifting

Your New Shifting Strategy

Connecting with your partner, as discussed in chapter 9, is the first step to calming the angry right brain fire. This helps her begin to *feel* a little better. The next part of your new strategy is *shifting*.

> **CONNECTING**
> Use *connection* to calm the relationship right brain (negative emotions).
>
> ▶ **SHIFTING**
> Use *shifting* to activate the logic left brain (positive emotions).
>
> **HONESTY**
> Use *honesty* to honor yourself and provide boundaries for your partner.
>
> **CONSEQUENCES**
> Allow *consequences* to help your partner learn.

Shifting

Part of the purpose in connecting is to begin to open the bridge (corpus callosum) from the right relationship brain to the left logic brain. Getting the rest of the way across the bridge is the next step and is the purpose of *shifting*.

Shifting is about activating the *thinking* left brain, and getting the information flowing back and forth across the bridge, checking in with both hemispheres. The best decisions are made when both hemisphere are working in harmony, and your partner will simply feel better. Positive emotions live over in the left hemisphere, so you want to get to them as soon as possible.

Just as you had a big role in the *connecting* step, you will have an equally big role in the *shifting* step. You need to do it because your partner will still be struggling and completely unaware of the brain battle. His focus is extremely narrow in the moment. One thought or line of thinking is in charge and he can't accept another line of argument or

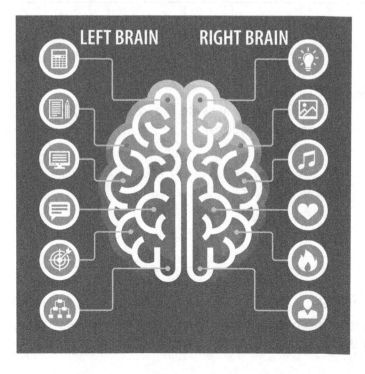

thinking. In fact, unknown to him, he believes that only one thing can be true at a time in his mind. Two opposite things cannot be true at the same time. It's your job to help him shift into more thinking. Let's take a look at the brain chart again. The left brain is where problem-solving is performed and finding options and ideas takes places. This is the exact spot you want to help guide your partner into.

Take a look at the right brain listing in the graphic on the opposite page, and think about how you would behave if you had only that hemisphere of your brain to use. Now look at the left brain list. Having access to everything on those lists by having the bridge open and traffic flowing between both hemispheres is the goal, and here are some technique to open the bridge and get traffic flowing.

▶ **With Words**

- "What do you *think* about that idea?"
- "Do you have any *thoughts* about that?"
- "What ideas do you have?"
- "Can you think of some options to solve this issue?"
- "Are there things you think I could be doing to help solve the issue?"
- "Who can you think of that could help us figure this out?"
- "Do you want to sit down with me and write some of these ideas on paper?"

One of the most effective methods is one from the book by Bill Eddy called *So, What's Your Proposal? Shifting High-Conflict People from Blaming to Problem-Solving in 30 Seconds*. In it he teaches a simple statement to use to shift others into the left brain. All it requires is this question: "So, what's your proposal?"

This question invites the bridge to open and requires the left brain to respond. Bottom line, it's activated *thinking*, and invited positivity and calmness into the conversation. Mr. Eddy explains further in the book that you may have to ask the question again or maybe a few times because the Complicated OS is used to its old patterns of hanging out in the right brain, so you will need to invite it to head back over to the left brain and you do this by asking again, "So, what's your proposal?" It keeps your partner *thinking*. It's a brilliant strategy! And it works!

The Goal
The goal of your words is to activate *thinking*, which opens the bridge to the left hemisphere. I encourage actually using the words "thinking" or "thoughts" to stimulate those actions. Other words also work.

What to Avoid
You may be a problem-solver by nature and you are used to solving problems at home, at work, and in many parts of your life, so it will be natural for you to want to solve the problem for your partner or generate ideas and options for her. This keeps the argument going and it actually *enables* bad behaviors to continue. Avoid your natural "fixing" and "problem-solving".

▶ **With Actions**
- Suggest that your partner write a list (another suggestion from Bill Eddy). The list can be about anything: how to tie a shoe, what to get everyone for Christmas, or a grocery list.

- Suggest some type of body movement like taking a walk with you.

- Suggest that your partner take some deep breaths with you.

- Suggest that you go do the shopping together or go out for dinner.

The Goal

The goal is to get both brain hemispheres activated through the use of some type of activity. Your partner might feel exhausted and overwhelmed at this point and want to be alone or take a nap. This is a good idea.

What to Avoid

Again, you'll want to avoid problem-solving for your partner. Your only job is to help by connecting and shifting.

Paying Attention

You may have to shift back and forth between connecting and shifting. You may have done a good job of connecting and shifting. Your partner has calmed down but is getting agitated again—a flare-up. Just watch for these and repeat the steps: connect and shift.

Honesty

One area the Complicated OS excels is in sniffing out dishonesty or not being authentic. There's also a lack of trust in others. When you aren't completely honest or authentic, your partner will know and it will cause him to become more agitated and stuck in right brain negative emotions again. The blaming, accusing and cursing may begin again, or he may revert back to feeling like a victim.

During an argument, your emotions might be running slightly more negative than usual and you might be feeling fear. Often, this causes us to avoid telling the truth because we're afraid it will cause the argument to grow. The best strategy is to continue connecting and shifting—do it from a genuine and authentic place.

Your honesty and authenticity will have two effects: it will help in the moment by not further enflaming her, and it will help her trust you. Commit to telling the truth no matter what.

CONNECTING
Use *connection* to calm the relationship right brain (negative emotions).

SHIFTING
Use *shifting* to activate the logic left brain (positive emotions).

▶ **HONESTY**
Use *honesty* to honor yourself and provide boundaries for your partner.

CONSEQUENCES
Allow *consequences* to help your partner learn.

Boundaries are usually pushed a lot with people who have a Complicated OS. They don't have a good grasp on boundaries for themselves, nor do they have your boundaries in mind, especially during an argument. If you're the type of person who struggles with having good boundaries for yourself, it's even harder for you with the Complicated OS because it wants to push those boundaries. Plus, your brain may be in fight, flight or freeze mode, so you're in a state of fear that convinces you to forget your new strategies and fearful of enforcing your boundaries.

What does it truly mean to have boundaries? It means having a set of rules for yourself that you enforce for how you will allow others to treat you. Your partner will push your boundaries (and push your buttons), so you need to be prepared by knowing what boundaries you do have and creating boundaries where they are lacking.

What happens when you don't enforce your boundaries? You grow frustrated, feel violated, feel helpless or hopeless. You actually enable your partner to stay sick. He needs you to have guard rails up so he knows he can't go beyond. Yes, he will bump into the rails, and it won't feel comfortable for you, but you help both of you by having guard rails in place and not moving them. When you're tempted to bend your boundaries, remind yourself that you can be most helpful by having good boundaries. This doesn't mean being completely inflexible, but it does mean that you won't allow yourself to be abused.

Consequences

The beauty of having and enforcing boundaries is that they result in consequences, which are especially beneficial to the Complicated OS. Consequences may be the only way the Complicated OS gets healthier in some cases. Think about your partner in a full-blown rage. She's smashed a chair into the wall. You make for the front door trying to escape, and she follows you at full speed, yelling, cursing and hitting you. Now you're in the front yard in a screaming match and the neighbors call the police. She gets arrested while you beg the police not to arrest her. As hard as it is to imagine, getting arrested—while inconvenient, expensive, and humiliating—may be the only thing that will stop her next time.

CONNECTING
Use *connection* to calm the relationship right brain (negative emotions).

SHIFTING
Use *shifting* to activate the logic left brain (positive emotions).

HONESTY
Use *honesty* to honor yourself and provide boundaries for your partner.

▶ **CONSEQUENCES**
Allow *consequences* to help your partner learn.

Don't be tempted to protect your partner from consequences that happen either from external sources or those that would happen in the natural course of events. Take a minute to think about this in your relationship. In what ways have you protected your partner from consequences? Has it helped or hindered? The answer is probably that it hindered.

Commit to standing aside when you feel the urge or need to protect your loved one from the pain of consequences. The pain is worth it in the long run.

CHAPTER 11

Be a Complicated Code Cracker

I n the movie, *The Imitation Game*, the plot centers on a team of cryptographers attempting to break codes created by the Enigma machine used by the Nazis during World War II to provide security for their messages. The Nazis were winning the war because no one could crack their codes. The price was high. Approximately four soldiers died every few minutes while the code remained uncracked. The team had an actual Enigma machine that was smuggled out of Berlin for them, but they didn't know the settings to decode messages. Their mission was to crack the code.

Each night, the Germans refreshed the settings, requiring the code breakers to start from scratch each morning. They had only eighteen hours each in day in which to crack the code. What frustrated them most was that the messages were floating around in the air for anyone to grab, but they were encrypted by the Nazis. With the resources they had, it would take twenty million years to go through the 159,000,000,000,000,000,000 possibilities. The pressure was on! Under tremendous stress and strain, they finally cracked it. With access to the Nazi's secret information, they were able to alert those who needed that information. They helped soldiers avoid traps that meant certain death and be in the right place at the right time to have the upper hand.

More than fourteen million lives were saved and the war was eventually won, not with the machinery of war—bombs, guns, artillery—but by six crossword enthusiasts with a commitment and steadfast resolve to crack the code.

Cracking the Complicated Code

You might view the Complicated OS like the crossword enthusiasts viewed the Enigma. Lots of messages in the air for you to grab, but they're encrypted by your partner. This chapter is designed to give you the codes to the Complicated OS. It's a look inside the mind at *his* thoughts and *her* thoughts. While we don't want to view your relationship as a war, it can become a war if you don't know the code. Wars end badly with a lot of wounds and destruction. Your relationship shouldn't end badly; it doesn't have to be destroyed. You just need to know the code. You have to know the mind of the person you're talking to.

It shouldn't take years and years to crack it, either. What follows is a shortcut; an inside look at what your partner is really saying instead of the actual words. The Complicated OS is a world of **opposites** and it pressures you to react and sometimes overreact. Instead, remember that the things being said and done are usually the opposite of what your partner really wants to say and do. He or she just doesn't have the skills to say and do them, at least not yet. So, to be successful you are required to do the **opposite** of:

- what you think is the logical thing to do
- what your emotions want you to do
- what you do with everyone else

Complicated Code Cracking

Coded Message: You NEVER listen to me!

Decoded Message: I feel disconnected. I don't feel heard. I need to be connected. You can help me by paying attention when I am talking to you, and by not interrupting me. Take a minute to focus on what I'm saying so I can feel connected.

Actions You Can Take:

Connect. In the moment you can say while giving direct eye contact and facing her directly, "Let's take five minutes to sit down together so I can hear what you have to say."

Boundary. "Then I have to go take a shower and get ready for work."

Listen without interruption for five minutes (don't go over). Give your full attention during that time and close it with, "I'm glad you shared that with me. I need to grab a shower and get to work on time. Let's plan to continue talking about this tonight after work or tomorrow if we're too tired."

Shift. Suggest that the two of you schedule a daily chat session at a certain time. "What would you think about scheduling a time together every day to spend 10-15 minutes talking? Do you like that idea? Or do you have other ideas you can think of? If you like it, do you want to come up with a few options for times we could meet?"

You don't want to be in the exhausting position of listening all the time. Instead of gasping for your attention and never feeling like she's getting enough, you've now built an expectation that you will spend time with her, which ultimately eases her anxiety, especially if you follow through and maintain consistency. If you have a scheduling conflict on a certain day, explain it in advance and reschedule. This serves the purpose of helping her look forward. Ask her if she'd like to find a new time to meet. Anything to keep her *thinking* and *looking forward* instead of getting stuck in the moment.

Don't defend yourself by saying that you listen to her a lot. Just focus on connecting and shifting.

Coded Message: You ALWAYS take EVERYONE else's side!

Decoded Message: I feel abandoned/disconnected when you defend your relationship with EVERYONE ELSE. I don't trust you. My brain divides people into all good and all bad. You can help me by not defending your relationship "right now" and explaining it to me "right now". Instead, take "right now" to help me feel better.

What You Shouldn't Say: "I wasn't taking sides." "I don't take sides." "You're the one who takes sides!"

Actions You Can Take: Your explanations (logic) are landing in her right brain—the side that doesn't have the job of using or translating logic. Without connection first, your logic can't reach his left logic brain because you haven't taken the time to connect, opening the bridge to left logic. Basically, you're wasting your time and only escalating his frustration and anxiety. Your words are a foreign language "right now". Instead, focus first on connecting with the right brain.

Connect. Use eye contact and focus on him, not the dishes, getting a drink from the fridge, looking at something on your computer. You can say, "Oh wow, I didn't realize how strongly you felt about this. Maybe we can take some time to talk about it. Seriously, I truly don't want to hurt you in any way nor do I want you to feel badly about this or about anything. Our relationship is my priority."

Shift. "Hey, do you want to take some time to *think* about some ways we can handle this so we can get it right, together?"

Connect and shift.

Coded Message: I want YOU to WANT know me! You care more about **everyone** else in the world. You couldn't care less about ME! You always put your "family" before ME!

Decoded Message: I feel empty and I need you to fill the emptiness. I feel out of control and my mind can't think of anything except this. You can help me by not walking away; by taking time to help me calm down.

What You Shouldn't Say: "Are you nuts?" "How many times do we have to go over this before you get it through your thick skull?" "I would care more about you if you didn't nag at me constantly about this!"

Actions You Can Take: You've been pushed to your limit and you're frustration, so you've resorted to anger. Not only are these words landing in her right brain and can't and reach the left logic brain, they're fanning the flames. You've added injury to an open wound. Instead, focus first on **connecting** to put out the fire.

Connect. Use eye contact and focus directly on her (the time investment is worth it). You can say, "I'm really sad that you feel badly about this. That's something I don't like for you to have to experience."

Shift. "Maybe you have some thoughts on how I can help you feel like more of a priority to me."

Connect and shift.

Coded Message: You ALWAYS make me feel bad! Why can't you at least make an attempt to understand me!?!?! You don't even WANT to help me! You don't CARE!

Decoded Message: I'm about to lose it and fly into Relationship Rage! I'm feeling desperately disconnected. I so badly want to feel better, but I have no idea how to do it myself. I feel like I can't breathe and I need oxygen—you are the oxygen! You can help me by not walking away. You can help me by giving me a hug, even if I tell you I don't want one.

What you shouldn't say: "Why do you say that?" "Why do I get blamed for everything?"

What you shouldn't do: Don't ignore the situation. Don't walk away. Don't defend yourself or fight back.

Actions You Can Take: Override what you're feeling, especially if you feel angry, defeated, or fed up. Tell yourself to connect and shift.

Connect. Grab his hand or put your arm around his shoulders (if he'll let you). Say with a calm, firm tone of voice, "You'd better believe I care. You are so important to me and I don't want you to *ever* feel like I don't.""

You don't always have to say something. It might be better to give a genuine smile, direct eye contact, gently walk to him and simply hold him. All of this is empathy and connection—exactly what his brain is craving.

Shift. "I have some ideas of things I can do to show you I care, but I'm also interested in hearing your thoughts and ideas."

Connect and shift.

Coded Event: Husband is texting his wife while he's at work. He wants to know if she's done working on the loan application they'd been discussing for two months and that she'd promised to finish that day with the help of her brother. She responded to his texts saying that they were working on it but it would take most of the day, instead of being finished by 1pm like she'd said earlier. This didn't stop him. The texting continued with a fury, one after the next. They weren't very nice. They were demanding, pushy, and slightly overly aggressive. She grew more and more upset with each text because her responses *explaining* the situation seemed to have no impact. He just kept asking the same questions and making the same demands. Her brother was angry, and he told other family members who also grew angry with the husband.

Decoded Event: The two-month delay in completing the loan application felt untrue to the husband. He felt like his wife was putting it off to hide something from him, and she waited until a day when he was at work to get it completed, which added to his suspicion that something devious was happening. He felt it as a threat to his connection with her. He felt left out, not included, and ultimately, disconnected and abandoned. Because he had to be at work, he had no control or influence except to text her. He was stuck in right brain negative emotions; the bridge to logic was closed. She thought he wanted answers and explanations. Instead, he wanted to feel connected and assured that she wasn't abandoning him.

His wife had specific reasons to handle it that particular day and they did have something to do with not wanting him involved. She wasn't trying to be mean, although that's what he accused her of being. Based on past negative experiences working with him on similar projects, she thought it was better to keep him out of the loop altogether.

The event was not based on just that day's events. It had been building for two months and culminated on that day.

Actions for a Better Outcome

Honesty. He may not have been happy about not being included, but honesty could have prevented the texting blizzard and ensuing chaos and frustration. He might have been a little upset about not being included in the application process, but it would have been better both in the short and long run. His trust in her was compromised. She could have said, "We've had a lot of difficulty in the past when we've worked on other applications. If it's okay with you, maybe I could complete it with the help of my brother while you're at work. Then, you can take a look at it after work and give your input. How does that sound? Any other ideas?"

Connect. During the texting blizzard, she reacted by giving logical explanations instead of connecting. His "upset" caused her to be "upset," too. Although her natural instinct was to be a conflict avoider, she felt obligated to respond to his texts. She could have said in her text message: "I love you. I'm sorry you're feeling yucky about this. I'm nearly finished with the application. Let's go over it together as soon as you get home, okay? Love you!"

Shift. "Hope you have a good day while you're working! Looking forward to hearing about your thoughts and ideas when you get home! Love you!"

Coded Event: A husband took his wife on a fabulous beach vacation to celebrate her 30th birthday. He surprised her with a visit to a spa for a massage and facial on her actual birthday, and they went out on a boat tour for the afternoon. After returning from the tour, they headed to their room for a late afternoon nap. When she woke up, he was watching television, so she spent the next hour watching with him. She asked what they were doing for dinner and he responded that it was her choice. Instead of the pleasant reaction he expected, she exploded. She let loose with a tirade with increasing volume and intensity. She was angry that he hadn't planned anything for her birthday; he didn't care how she felt; he didn't care that it was her 30th birth-day—a special one; he was an a-hole who had no feelings; and on and on. Every time he tried to answer her, he strug-gled to find words, and the words he uttered were cut in half as if she had a sword. He couldn't win. He smacked his forehead with his hand at one point, looking incredulous at what was happening, which escalated her anger exponen-tially. He got off the bed and walked away from her into the bathroom. Finally, the wife stormed out of the room, slam-ming the door behind her. She walked around the resort for twenty or thirty minutes before walking into a restaurant where she had dinner alone. The husband sat bewildered in the room having no idea what just happened. One minute they were watching TV and the next they were in a def-con 5 fight. His heart was racing, head pounding, and he was shaking. After twenty minutes or so, he went around the resort looking for her but was unsuccessful. Finally, he spot-ted her walking.

Decoded Event: Long before they left for the trip, she be-gan fantasizing about her first romantic beach vacation, complete with dinner for two right on the beach. She'd been on the resort website where she discovered that they offered a special private romantic dinner for two on the beach. It wasn't offered as part of their vacation package; her husband would have to request it and pay an extra fee for it. She fully anticipated that her romantic, thoughtful husband would surely do this for her because it was a mile stone birthday, and it was her first beach vacation.

He knew nothing of her online research or hope for the private birthday dinner. He thought he was being sweet by letting her choose a restaurant for her birthday dinner. Her Complicated OS translated that as him not caring enough about her to actually plan something special. And that triggered her fear of disconnection, sending her into an instant rage. Verbal vomit spewed forth. She didn't hear a word he said. Nothing registered in her brain. She was fully stuck in negative right-brain emotions with zero access to logic. She felt epic devastation and anger. When her emotions were too overwhelming, her Complicated OS sent her on the escape route.

The husband couldn't have anticipated what was in his wife's mind or her expectations for the evening—he's not a mind reader. The conflict erupted so quickly; he was completely taken by surprise. His operating system, although it was healthy, did its job. Once it sensed fear, it triggered fight, flight, or freeze, and he was quickly rocketed into his natural fear-state—a flight/freezer. He couldn't move, couldn't talk, couldn't think. He felt like his head was going to explode and he wanted to be anywhere but in that room and in that situation.

The scenario was set up in the months, days, hours, and minutes leading up to the event. The dinner wasn't the issue even though you might think it was. The need to feel connected and the feeling of disconnect was the issue.

Actions for a Better Outcome

Connect. These types of confrontations are the most difficult to handle because of the surprise factor. The agitation and anxiety started in her mind during that hour they watched TV together. He thought that spending time together on the tour, the special spa surprise, and giving her the choice of restaurants for dinner was romantic and loving. He probably thought he was connecting. Unfortunately, he was in a no-win situation and at a disadvantage after it started.

He wouldn't have the chance to even think about over-riding his natural reaction of freezing and wanting to flee the room. In this particular situation, it was his first experience of this happening with his wife, or frankly, with anyone ever. If it had been something he'd dealt with in the past, he may have been able to override the natural fear-state and use connecting words with a soft voice, eye contact and body language that showed he was paying attention.

He erred by smacking his hand on his forehead and giving an incredulous look. Walking away from her into the bathroom furthered her feeling of disconnect. Going to look for her was good. It let her feel that he wanted to connect with her. Even though she was still grouchy and biting, she slowly began to calm down as they walked together and he grabbed her hand. Connecting.

It's hard to imagine that anyone should have to put up with such behavior. Like I said at the beginning of the book and repeated it often throughout, empathy is required. It may not seem fair that the partner should have to "cave in" to demands, accusations, insults, and adapt behavior and natural reactions. Is it fair? Not really. Does it work? Most of the time, it does.

Cracking the complicated code takes a lot of practice, but it's possible to do!

You can find more examples of cracking the complicated code on my website: http://www.unhookedmedia.com/complicated-relationships-form/.

CHAPTER 12

Addressing Other Concerns
and Unique Questions

The response I get from many friends and acquaintances when I describe what this book is about and its intent—to save relationships—is, "Aren't these the relationships that should go to divorce court?" "Why would anyone want to stay in a relationship that is so difficult?" "Why not end it and start over with someone who is easy to live with?" "Why would you want to put yourself through the hard work trying to salvage it when a successful outcome is slim?"

I explain that divorce or some type of relationship termination doesn't have to be the only option. Sure, it's hard work adapting your behavior and learning a new management strategy, but why not give it a try? What if it works?

I'm not one to give up easily and neither should you. An incident my brother encountered reinforced this for me. In 2007, at the age of 43, an accident left him with a traumatic brain injury. He was strapped to a bed with round-the-clock supervision because he walked into walls, was combative, and his language was unintelligible. As his newly court-appointed legal guardian and conservator, I was responsible for his care and decisions. After scouring the country for a treatment facility that could help restore his brain back to health, a top-notch hospital said they would help him and asked me to send his medical records right away. A few days later they called to say that he had sustained an injury that was beyond repair. He would never recover; he would never change. They suggested that I find a lock-down Alzheimer's unit where he could spend the rest of his life. Unfortunately, I could not get a facility anywhere to open their doors to him, so he was shifted between a variety of facilities for a couple of years. But, in less than five years, not only was he walking and talking as if nothing had happened, he was working full-time at the best job he'd ever had, and had almost no after-effects from the brain injury. That's why I don't give up, and hopefully it will give you some encouragement to not give up either. Yes, relationships are different from a brain injury, but at least in your situation, you have the tools within your grasp to make changes and possibly make a difference.

The rest of this chapter focuses on the most frequently asked questions and common concerns about complicated relationships.

Two Sides to the Coin

As exhausting and frustrating as these relationships can be, you've also experienced something extraordinary with your partner. We tend to forget that this person who can confuse and frustrate us is the same person who has incredible empathy for others or a tender sweetness that is raw, powerful, and very real. Is it that she has two sides? A dark side and a light side? I don't see it that way and here's why you shouldn't either: She is one whole person whose brain developed down the complicated relationship path instead of the healthy one. Know this: she did not choose it, didn't create it, doesn't even know she has it, and wouldn't want it if she knew she had it.

He would describe himself as a compassionate person who loves deeply. This is true. He loves to be happy and feel good, but the Complicated OS gets in the way sometimes and makes life deeply painful, so painful that the emotions have to purge from his body to the outside world. It's not intentional. He has a surplus of empathy for others, but not so much for himself.

Why does this matter? It matters because you are in a unique position to make a difference in someone's life. We talk in society about making a difference and helping others have a more positive life. Now, you have the opportunity to use your new Complicated OS skills to make a difference not in a stranger's life, but in the life of the person you fell in love with and has all the good stuff in place. With a little outside help from you, and possibly some professional assistance, you may be able to help turn the Complicated OS into a healthy OS. You can help lift the blanket to reveal the good stuff.

Not only will both you and your partner benefit, but if you have children, they will be the recipients of healthier parenting and role modeling.

Below is an actual statement from someone who took the challenge to stay with the relationship, adapt the Complicated OS strategy, and find success:

> "Sticking by my wife through the hard times after learning about her Complicated OS was the most gratifying thing I've done in my life. The result was a good relationship. It certainly was hard for her and hard for me, but I loved her and I saw that under the anger, jealousy, and hostility was a profound pain and something was driving it that wasn't present in other people. I was fortunate that she was open to going to therapy and she was will-

ing to be honest about her problems. She put her ego aside and decided to be vulnerable and work on it. Either you love the person and you're going to put in the effort, or you get stuck in arguments, conflict, rage, and bouts of depression . . . both hers and my own. But it's not a one-sided thing. It takes two. Why throw away a relationship that actually has the potential to succeed and last a lifetime with an adjustment on my part and work on her part . . . and mine? Yes, it was frustrating and hard to stop falling back into the old patterns, but complicated relationships tend to be the ones that can give you the highest highs and your lowest lows. If you can eliminate your lowest lows, then wow! She's definitely a keeper!"

Forgiveness

If you've been the recipient of a few f-bombs, personal attacks, name-calling, scratching, hitting, or getting thrown under the bus, you know how hard it is to even like this person, let alone forgive them. First, forgiveness is for you. If you don't let it go, it will hold you back. Second, forgiveness helps your partner move on and heal. Shame is a big part of the Complicated OS. When you don't forgive, the already present shame receives another layer of shame. Third, your act of forgiveness shows your partner a different way of relating with other humans. The Complicated OS tends to hold grudges. If you show a different way, your partner just might pick up on it.

Is this a Mental Health Issue?

Possibly.

When we think of mental health, we think about diagnosis and medication; however, this is not an "illness" that is "fixed" with medication. Why not? It's not a chemical imbalance in the brain. When we think of "mental health," our first thought typically goes to medication. It's true that the Complicated OS creates a lot of anxiety, and some people take anti-anxiety medications. But, this is a decision for a licensed mental health professional who is authorized to prescribe such medications.

Often, help from a mental health professional is ideal; however, part of the reason I wrote this book is in recognition of the reality that many, many people do not get that type or help either due to lack of available services, affordability, biases, or other reasons. Getting outside assistance from a mental health professional is ideal and should be pursued. In the absence of outside assistance or as a supplement to it, this book is designed to provide an understanding of the brain processes of both of you, and suggestions for things you can try.

Avoid is labeling or "diagnosing" your partner. Instead, walk beside him or her through the journey of change. Don't demonize your partner—it only adds shame and induces flame.

Trauma often plays a huge role in the Complicated OS. The removal of trauma through therapy can clear a lot of "ugly" behaviors from the Complicated OS.

Does My Partner Need Therapy? How Do I Get Him or Her to Go?

Your partner may not believe that therapy or any type of counseling is needed. This is an area of great resistance because he or she may not believe that they're the one with a problem. And they're right, at least partially. Just as alcoholism is a family disease, this is a relationship (couples) disorder. Both of you will benefit from getting help from a licensed professional with the right expertise.

Have a conversation with your partner that focuses on improving your relationship together. Explain that there is help for couples who take a pro-active approach to allowing someone else help you shift your relationship into calmness and stability. Explain that you know you need to make changes and you need to make some together.

The thought of seeing a psychologist, therapist, or other mental health professional can be scary to your partner, and maybe to you as well. The way I like to think about it is exactly like any diagnosis of a physical ailment, such as diabetes, lupus, or many others. I am not trained to be my own doctor. I don't have the training, nor do I have access to the right diagnostic testing or prescriptions, but the medical community does. I take great care to find a doctor who specializes in my ailment to get the best treatment possible with the goal of reducing my symptoms or pain, and extending my life.

It's no different with emotional health. I am not trained to be my own therapist (although there are many things I can do on my own to help with healing). I don't have the training or expertise, but there are those who do.

Present it as a "together" endeavor; a "we" venture. Both of you can research professionals in your area and pick one from each list (unless you're comfortable going with the one your partner chooses). A good therapist/counselor will have training and/or expertise in at least some of these areas: anxiety, trauma, PTSD, complex trauma, BPD, emotion regulation, or personality disorders. Look for someone who teaches Dialectical Behavior Therapy™ (DBT), specifically designed to help people get emotions under control;

to think about two opposite things being true at the same time; to learn new skills for having better relationships; and other skills.

If your partner will not go to therapy, it might be a good idea for you to go alone anyway so you can get outside perspective about your relationship and make the decisions you need to make for yourself.

If you are not in a financial position to pay for outside assistance, see if you can find local organizations that provide free or reduced-rate therapy. Some churches have counseling centers. While I believe that faith can play a big part in saving these relationships, I'm a bit cautious about seeking counseling from a clergy member. I don't altogether discourage it, but caution is suggested. These are the most difficult relationships, and many people don't understand them. You want to avoid bad advice from someone who doesn't understand the Complicated OS.

Random & Miscellaneous Helpful Hints

- **Pet Connections**. Pets, especially dogs, can be a big help to someone with a Complicated OS. They provide a source of connection and stability. They don't hold grudges, nor do they judge, place blame, or provide shame.

- **Contracts**. Contracts can be extremely helpful in the complicated relationship. They provide structure, boundaries, rewards, and consequences. They give a point of reference that just might be the "one" thing that stops bad behavior. Don't suggest that your partner have a contract. Instead, suggest that both of you have contracts for things you want to do together in your relationship. The contract can be about any issue you want to resolve, problem you want to conquer, or goal you want to set. For example, if you struggle with saying no, write it in a contract with your partner. If your partner has a hard time with jealousy or throwing things, write it in a contract. Be sure to make it non-negotiable. You can find a sample contract to download and print for free on my website at: http://www.unhookedmedia.com/complicated-relationships-form/

- **Identify**. A positive way to connect with your partner and avoid defensiveness is to identify your own struggles. For example:

  - "I struggle with overreacting sometimes, too."

  - "I have a hard time with _____."

  - "I'm not perfect either."

  Identify your own weaknesses and vulnerabilities in some way. It will show that you can identify, even a little, with him or her, but more importantly, your partner will feel a little less "bad" knowing that he or she isn't always the bad guy.

- **Rage**. You can't begin to comprehend the split second nature of rage associated with the Complicated OS. When you hear that someone "snapped," they, in fact, did just that. You might think it's intentional or they have control over it. Know this: they don't. That doesn't make it okay. Knowing this should have the effect of motivating you to utilize your best connecting and shifting skills to help your partner avoid rage. **Rage is best handled by a mental health professional.**

Some have explained that even though they had no intention whatsoever of throwing the glass in their hand, jumping out of the moving car, or hitting you, the overwhelming pain and anxiety of not getting you to connect with them in that moment caused a snap that was not planned or even thought about. In one such case, during an argument during a car ride about a girl's jealousy over her boyfriend ignoring her at an event, and talking to other girl's there, the girl jumped out of the car at 40 miles per hour and rolled down the pavement. She ended up with a broken bone, lots of road rash, and a few months of doctor visits, casts, and wound care. When interviewed about it, she explained her thoughts that night:

> "As usual, I was angry over my boyfriend flirting with other girls; at least my mind believed he was flirting. On the ride home, I accused him of it. He denied it. I escalated to the next stage of anger and disconnection. It went back and forth a few times, with rage building with each exchange. That rage came from intense pain. I wanted him to ease the pain, but he defended his actions and fought back instead. At one point, the thought of jumping out of the car crossed my mind. It wasn't about killing myself. Far from it. My mind had two thoughts: 1) I'll sure show him! and 2) this is just too painful and I need something to ease the pain. As strange as this may sound, because of those two thoughts, I had absolutely no intention of jumping out of that car. I'm a very logical person and logic told me it would hurt or kill me. The next thing I knew, I was rolling down the pavement. I'd said something to him in the continued argument and he yelled back. That

did it. Without thinking, in a split second I was rolling down the street. I could easily have hit my head on a curb and died or suffered terrible injuries. It was terrifying for both of us. Neither of us understood what was happening, why it had happened, how we got there, or what to do next. I eventually ended up in a trauma center that night—very expensive and humiliating. The only good outcome of the episode was it prompted me to take down my walls a little and reveal to my family that I was in so much pain and I didn't know why. I'd been in counseling for a few months but wasn't seeing any positive changes. This episode prompted me to find a therapist with experience in trauma treatment and emotion regulation. The healing began and I can proudly say that even though it took more time, and a few more bad experiences, I'm now free of the toxic relationship that both of us had created and my Complicated OS has progressed to a healthy operating system. It is possible. "

- **Faith**. Many who deal with the Complicated OS have found comfort and anxiety reduction through their spiritual life. I'm not here to push religion; rather, I'm passing along information that others have reported to be helpful in their transition or recovery. They've explained that a connection with God provides a "connection," the very thing they crave most.

- **Substance Abuse and Self-Harm**. Often, alcohol, prescription, and non-prescription drugs are used to numb pain and quell anxiety. It makes sense that someone with a Complicated OS would frequently use substances or medication for these purposes because of the anxiety and pain that comes with their OS. Self-harm is sometimes present also. Even though I've watched every episode of *Intervention*, I'm still not qualified to advise you on handling substance abuse and self-harm, other than to direct you to resources in your community and online where you can find help for both you and your partner. See the Resources section.

- **What Not to Say.** Telling your partner that he or she is damaged goods, complicated, mental, psycho, psychotic, a psych case, crazy, horrible, borderline, BPD, a lunatic, an idiot, a sociopath, belongs in a psych ward or a straight jacket, or anything derogative is a very, very, extremely bad idea. Don't do it.

- **Expectations.** Just because you adapt your behavior and see some improvements, the Complicated OS hasn't been cured. You will experience small victories along with setbacks, some small and others monumental, but you stick to your plan. Time spent in trauma treatment or other skill-based therapies increase the successes.

- **Judgment.** Your partner doesn't want to feel judged. He or she is keenly aware of judgment and already feels judged by almost everyone.

- **Openness and Vulnerability.** Be open about your strengths and weaknesses and encourage your partner to do the same. Be vulnerable with each other. One caveat—don't betray your partner's weaknesses to anyone. Trust is key, so you don't want to comprise the trust you've built. Celebrate the strengths and grow through the weaknesses.

- **Biting Your Tongue.** A great temptation you'll face is that you want to respond or reply to everything your partner comes up with. You don't need to.

In fact, it's better to bite your tongue. He or she isn't always asking for a solution or for you to be a problem-solver. Just nod and show you're paying attention. It's easier for both of you. This is what it means to "walk beside" your partner.

- **Tornadoes, Blizzards, and Hurricanes**. Metaphorically speaking, you've probably experienced tornadoes, blizzards, and hurricanes. Sometimes it's in person and sometimes it's by phone, text, email, or social media. A text blizzard doesn't need to dominate and destroy your day. That blizzard is about your partner feeling immensely disconnected "right now" and desperately needing to connect. So, do the same strategy "right now" that you do with everything else. When you respond, use *connecting* language to calm the fire in the right brain. Then use *shifting* language to get him or her focused on something else, or focused on the future. You should be able to do this within the space of 2-3 text messages. Then, calmly reply that you are signing off because you have to go back to work, get to sleep, etc.

  Do the same with an in-person tornado or Category 5 hurricane. *Connect*, then *shift*. Be honest (boundaries). If you've set up a special "together time" each day, you should be able to avoid a lot of "weather." Keeping secrets is sure to bring on a lot of weather. Commit to being honest, always. It's a gift you can give your partner.

- **Boundaries**. This might be the most important and gratifying thing you can do for both of you. Once you experience the empowerment of boundaries, you'll be motivated to use them more. It's another gift you can give your partner.

Exit Strategies

When I conceptualized this book, an entire chapter was created to developing an exit strategy when the complicated relationships doesn't work out. However, during the writing process, I've realize that my strategies are perfect and will work for everyone. Just kidding! In honesty, I'm reluctant to offer advice on exiting because it is the most dangerous time in a complicated relationship.

If you reach a decision to leave the relationship or you have any fears about harm to yourself or to your partner, please seek advice from a mental health professional and develop a good plan to make it peaceful and to avoid violence of any kind. Several resources are included in the Resource section to help you.

Final Thoughts

I wish both of you my very best. Please know that this book doesn't have all the answers, nor do I have all the answers, but I hope you have found some measure of relief and direction through these pages. I've learned from the very best in the field—leaders like Bill Eddy, Blaise Aguirre, Randi Kreger, Amanda Smith, Shari Manning, and others—conducted my own research, practiced it in my own relationships, and taught others to use it in theirs. I've attempted to write in a non-clinical way and tried to personalize it so you can apply it to your own scenarios and struggles. I hope it's made sense.

Perfection will never be attained, but long-term stability can be. Stay strong and remind yourself that your partner is a unique, hurting human with loads of amazing qualities (even if it's hard to see them sometimes) and so are you. Remember to do the opposite of what you feel like doing and are used to doing.

Come back to the book every once in a while to remind yourself what to do, refresh your batteries, and get unhooked!

I would love to hear your stories. In my view, they're all successes because even those we consider failures are opportunities to grow. Please reach out to me at megan@unhookedbooks.com anytime. I'm a real person who will respond to you myself.

 Resources like sample contracts, videos, and others materials can be found at: http://www.unhookedmedia.com/complicated-relationships-form/.

Continue with confidence!

RESOURCES

CRISIS HELP

The National Domestic Violence Hotline
www.thehotline.org/
1-800-799-7233

National Suicide Prevention Lifeline
1-800-273-8255
suicidepreventionlifeline.org

Substance Abuse Self-Help Groups
findtreatment.samhsa.gov/locator/link-focSelfGP

Faith-based Substance Abuse Self-Help Groups
celebraterecovery.com/

WELLNESS PLANNERS

Daily DBT Wellness Planner
The Dialectical Behavior Therapy™ Wellness Planner
by Amanda L. Smith, LMSW
http://unhookedbooks.com/the-dialectical-behavior-
therapy-wellness-planner/

Daily Wellness Planner
The 9 Daily Habits of Healthy People
by Melanie Lane, MD
http://unhookedbooks.com/the-9-daily-habits-of-healthy-
people/

BOOKS

BIFF: Quick Responses to High-Conflict People, Their Hostile Email, Personal Attacks, and Social Media Meltdowns by Bill Eddy, LCSW, Esq.

Stop Walking on Eggshells by Randi Kreger

Splitting: Protecting Yourself While Divorcing Someone with Borderline or Narcissistic Personality Disorder by Bill Eddy, LCSW, Esq., and Randi Kreger

Boundaries: When to Say Yes and How to Say No by Henry Cloud and John Townsend

Men, Women & Worthiness by Brené Brown

So, What's Your Proposal? Shifting High-Conflict People from Blaming to Problem-Solving in 30 Seconds by Bill Eddy, LCSW, Esq.

ONLINE SUPPORT

Get Unhooked
Online courses for partners of someone with a "Complicated Operating System"
http://unhookedbooks.com/bait-switch/

Personality Disorder Awareness Network
Information and support
pdan.org

Welcome to Oz
Support for partners
bpdcentral.com/support-groups

DBT Online Classes
teresalynne.net

Find a Dialectical Behavior Therapist
behavioraltech.org/resources/crd.cfm

ACKNOWLEDGMENTS

Thanks to my parents for giving me the right ingredients for successful future relationships. Thanks to my husband for being kind, sweet, encouraging, and always willing to listen and problem solve. Thanks to my kids for learning about being a family, together. Thanks to those who trusted me with their stories and experiences. Thanks to my friends, Chris Francis and Jon Webster, for being authentic. Thanks to my influencers, who opened the doors of understanding about the most difficult of difficult relationships: Bill Eddy, Randi Kreger, and Betsy Van Tuinen. Thanks to Allan Koritzinsky for giving me extra insight, helping me close the gaps, and cheering me on. Thanks to Cathy Broberg, an amazing editor who slogged through the muck with me, and to Victoria Simons, a proofreader with a bright future. You both made my work shine. You have all paid it forward.

P.S. A special thanks to everyone who produces reality television. You've provided a world-class opportunity to observe the patterns of the Complicated Operating System.

ABOUT THE AUTHOR

Megan Hunter is a leading expert on the topic of complicated relationships — the most difficult of "difficult" relationships. She is a frequent speaker to legal, business, mental health, parenting and relationship groups in Australia, the U.S., and Canada.

As CEO and founder of Unhooked Media, her work focuses on multi-media publishing in the area of complicated relationships and high-conflict disputes. She is co-founder of the High Conflict Institute along with author and speaker, Bill Eddy, LCSW, Esq.

She holds an M.B.A. from the University of Phoenix and a Bachelor's of Business and Economics from Chadron State College, Chadron, Nebraska. She served as President of the Arizona Chapter of the Association of Family & Conciliation Courts, the Arizona Family Support Council and Nebraska Child Support Enforcement Association. More recently, she served on the Arizona Board of Psychologist Examiners and the Advisory Board of the Personality Disorder Awareness Network.

She was given the Outstanding Contribution Award from the Arizona Association of Family & Conciliation Courts in 2010 and the Friend of Psychology Award from the Arizona Psychological Association in 2006.

She lives in Arizona and is married with three children and five stepchildren.

Visit her website at: www.UnhookedMedia.com.

More Great Books from
Unhooked Books

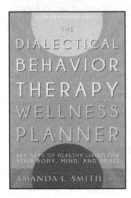

The Complicated Relationships Publisher

Available in paperback and in ebook (digital)
format from booksellers
everywhere

Visit our online bookstore at
www.unhookedbooks.com
Or call 1-888-986-4665

CPSIA information can be obtained at www.ICGtesting.com
Printed in the USA
LVOW04s0802180515

438812LV00002B/2/P